"IT'S TIME..."
"TOUYA, LOOK
AT THE SKY!"
LU POINTED UPWARDS
AT A STRANGE ARC OF
BRIGHT LIGHT IN THE SKY.
YAE STARED UPWARDS
WITH WIDE EYES.
"DID THE SKY SPLIT?"

FEW SMALL RUMBLINGS THAT
PERSISTED IN THE BACKGROUND.

In Another World With My Smartphone 18

LU'S WALTRAUTE
SWAPPED OUT TO ITS
C-UNIT AND BEGAN SWIFTLY
SUPPORTING THE OTHERS
ACROSS THE BATTLEFIELD.
THE C-UNIT WAS A
LONG-RANGE CANNON ON
THE RIGHT SHOULDER,
ALLOWING LU TO SNIPE
THE ENEMIES ONE
AFTER THE OTHER.

"I'LL SUPPORT YOU FROM BEHIND!"

YAE'S SCHWERTLEITE, HILDE'S SIEGRUNE, AND ELZE'S GERHILDE CHARGED OUT ONTO THE BEACH. THE FRAME GEARS BEHIND THEM, PILOTED BY SOLDIERS FROM ALL AROUND THE EASTERN CONTINENT, TOOK UP THEIR ARMS AND CHARGED AS WELL.

In Another World With My Smartphone

Patora Fuyuhara
illustration·Eiji Usatsuka

Luli

The fourth of Touya's summoned Heavenly Beasts. She is the Azure Monarch, the ruler of dragons. She often clashes with Kohaku due to her condescending personality.

Kougyoku

The third of Touya's summoned Heavenly Beasts. She is the Flame Monarch, ruler of feathered things. Though her appearance is flashy and extravagant, she's actually quite cool and collected.

Sango and Kokuyou

The second of Touya's summoned Heavenly Beasts. They are the Black Monarch, two in one. The rulers of scaled beasts. They can freely manipulate water. Sango is a tortoise, and Kokuyou is a snake. Sango is a female, and Kokuyou is a male (but he's very much a female at heart).

Kohaku

The first of Touya's summoned Heavenly Beasts. She's the White Monarch, the ruler of beasts, the guardian of the West and a beautiful White Tiger. She can create devastating shockwaves, and also change size at will.

High Rosetta

Terminal Gynoid in charge of the Workshop, one of the Babylon relics. She's called Rosetta for short. Her Airframe Serial Number is #27. For whatever reason, she's the most reliable of the bunch.

Francesca

Terminal Gynoid in charge of the Hanging Garden, one of the Babylon relics. She's called Cesca for short. Her Airframe Serial Number is #23. She likes to tell very inappropriate jokes.

Mochizuki Moroha

The God of Swords. Claims to be Touya's older sister. She trains and advises the knights of Brunhild. She's gallant and brave, but also a bit of an airhead at times.

Mochizuki Karen

The God of Love. Claims to be Touya's older sister. She stays in Brunhild because she says she needs to catch a servile god, but doesn't really do all that much in the way of hunting him. She's a total pain in the butt.

Pamela Noel

Terminal Gynoid in charge of the Tower, one of the Babylon relics. She's called Noel for short and wears a jersey. Her Airframe Serial Number is #25. She sleeps all the time, and eats lying down. Her tremendous laziness means she doesn't do all that much.

Preliora

Terminal Gynoid in charge of the Rampart, one of the Babylon relics. She's called Liora for short and wears a blazer. Her Airframe Serial Number is #20. She's the oldest of the Babylon Gynoids, and would attend to the... personal night-time needs of Doctor Babylon herself. She has no experience with men.

Fredmonica

Terminal Gynoid in charge of the Hangar, one of the Babylon relics. She's called Monica for short. Her Airframe Serial Number is #28. She's a funny little hard worker who has a bit of a casual streak. She's a good friend of Rosetta, and is the Gynoid with the most knowledge of the Frame Gears.

Bell Flora

Terminal Gynoid in charge of the Alchemy Lab, one of the Babylon relics. She's called Flora for short and wears a nurse outfit. Her Airframe Serial Number is #21. A nurse with dangerously big boobs and even more dangerous medicines.

Doctor Regina Babylon

An ancient genius from a lost civilization, reborn into an artificial body that resembles a small girl. She is the "Babylon" that created the many artifacts and forgotten technologies scattered around the world today. Her Airframe serial number is #29. she remained in stasis for five-thousand years before finally being awakened.

Atlantica

Terminal Gynoid in charge of the Research Lab, one of the Babylon relics. She's called Tica for short. Her Airframe serial number is #22. Of the Babylon Numbers, she is the one who best embodies Doctor Babylon's inappropriately perverse side.

Lileleparshe

Terminal Gynoid in charge of the Storehouse, one of the Babylon relics. She's called Parshe for short and wears a shrine maiden outfit. Her Airframe Serial Number is #26. She's tremendously clumsy, even if she's just trying to help. The amount of stuff she ruins is troublingly high.

Irisfam

Terminal Gynoid in charge of the Library, one of the Babylon relics. She's called Fam for short and wears a school uniform. Her Airframe Serial Number is #24. She's a total book fanatic and hates being interrupted when she's reading.

Character Profiles

Elze Silhoueska

One of Touya's fiancees.
The elder of the twin sisters saved by Touya some time ago. A ferocious melee fighter, she makes use of gauntlets in combat. Her personality is fairly to-the-point and blunt. She can make use of Null fortification magic, specifically the spell [Boost]. She loves spicy foods.

Yumina Urnea Belfast

One of Touya's fiancees.
Princess of the Belfast Kingdom. She was twelve years old in her initial appearance, and her eyes are heterochromatic. The right is blue, while the left is green. She has mystic eyes that can discern the true character of an individual. She has three magical aptitudes: Earth, Wind, and Darkness. She's also extremely proficient with a bow and arrow. She fell in love with Touya at first sight.

Mochizuki Touya

A highschooler who was accidentally murdered by God. He's a no-hassle kind of guy who likes to go with the flow. He's not very good at reading the atmosphere, and typically makes rash decisions that bite him in the ass. His mana pool is limitless, he can flawlessly make use of every magical element, and he can cast any Null spell that he wants. He's currently the Grand Duke of Brunhild.

Sushie Urnea Ortlinde

One of Touya's fiancees.
She was ten years old in her initial appearance. Her nickname is Sue. The niece of Belfast's king, and Yumina's cousin. Touya saved her from being attacked on the road. She has an innocently adventurous spirit.

Lucia Leah Regulus

One of Touya's fiancees.
The Third Princess of the Regulus Empire, she's Yumina's age. She fell in love with Touya when he saved her during a coup. She likes to fight with twin blades, and she's on good terms with Yumina.

Kokonoe Yae

One of Touya's fiancees.
A samurai girl from the far eastern land of Eashen, a country much like Japan. She tends to repeat herself and speak formally, she does. Yae is quite a glutton, eating more than most normal people would dare touch. She's a hard worker, but can sometimes slack off. Her family runs a dojo back in Eashen, and they take great pride in their craft. It's not obvious at first, but her boobs are pretty big.

Linze Silhoueska

One of Touya's fiancees.
The younger of the twin sisters saved by Touya some time ago. She wields magic, specifically from the schools of Light, Water, and Fire. She finds talking to people difficult due to her own shy nature, but she is known to be surprisingly bold at times. Rumors say she might be the kind of girl who enjoys male on male romance... She loves sweet foods.

Paula

A stuffed toy bear animated by years upon years of the [Program] spell. She's the result of two-hundred years of programmed commands, making her seem like a fully aware living being. Paula... Paula's the worst!

Sakura

A mysterious girl Touya rescued in Eashen. She had lost her memories, but has now finally gotten them back. Her true identity is Farnese Forneus, daughter of the Xenoahs Overlord. Currently living a peaceful life in Brunhild, and she has joined the ranks of Touya's fiancees.

Leen

One of Touya's fiancees.
Former Clan Matriarch of the Fairies, she now serves as Brunhild's Court Magician. She claims to be six-hundred-and-twelve years old, but looks tremendously young. She can wield every magical element except Darkness, meaning her magical proficiency is that of a genius. Leen is a bit of a light-hearted bully.

Hildegard Minas Lestia

One of Touya's fiancees.
First Princess of the Knight Kingdom Lestia. Her swordplay talents earned her a reputation as a 'Knight Princess'. Touya saved her life when she was attacked by a group of Phrase, and she's loved him ever since. She's a good friend of Yae, and she stammers a bit when flustered.

IN ANOTHER WORLD WITH MY SMARTPHONE: VOLUME 18
by Patora Fuyuhara

Translated by Andrew Hodgson
Edited by DxS
English Cover & Lettering by Carl Vanstiphout

Copyright © 2019 Patora Fuyuhara
Illustrations by Eiji Usatsuka

Original Japanese edition published in 2019 by Hobby Japan
This English edition is published by arrangement with Hobby Japan, Tokyo

English translation © 2019 J-Novel Club LLC

Find more books like this one at www.j-novel.club!

Managing Director: Samuel Pinansky
Light Novel Line Manager: Chi Tran
Managing Editor: Jan Mitsuko Cash
Managing Translator: Kristi Fernandez
QA Manager: Hannah N. Carter
Marketing Manager: Stephanie Hii

ISBN: 978-1-7183-5017-5
Printed in Korea
First Printing: October 2021
10 9 8 7 6 5 4 3 2 1

Contents

The Story So Far!

Mochizuki Touya, wielding a smartphone customized by God himself, continues to live his life in a new world. After many adventures, Touya, now Grand Duke of a small nation named Brunhild, has joined forces with the other world leaders. Why? To stop the incoming extradimensional threat known as the Phrase. These merciless invaders from another world will stop at nothing until they get what they desire. As Touya continued to investigate potential ways to repel this threat, he found himself falling into another world entirely. This Reverse World was like a mirrored version of the world he knew, and relied on a mysterious mechanical technology known as the Gollems. Now, the fate of two worlds may hang in the balance...

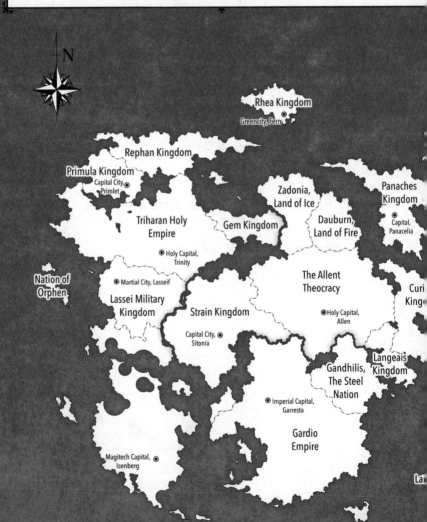

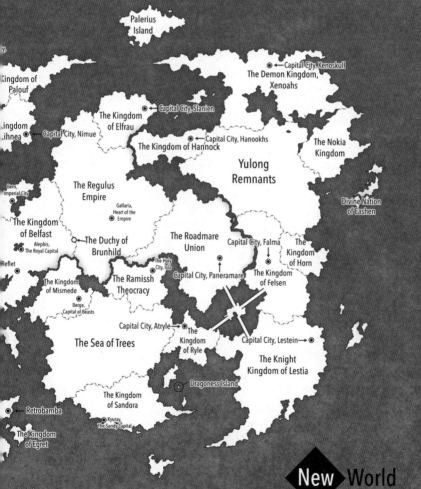

Palerius
Island

Kingdom of
Palouf

Capital City, Xenoskull
The Demon Kingdom,
Xenoahs

The Kingdom
of Elfrau — Capital City, Slanien

Kingdom
Ihnea — Capital City, Nimue

Capital City, Hanookhs
The Kingdom of Hannock

The Nokia
Kingdom

Yulong
Remnants

Bern,
Imperial City

The Regulus
Empire

Gallaria,
Heart of the
Empire

Divine Nation
of Eashen

The Kingdom
of Belfast

Alephis,
The Royal Capital

The Duchy of
Brunhild

The Roadmare
Union

Capital City, Falma

The
Kingdom
of Horn

Reflet

The Kingdom
of Mismede

The Ramissh
Theocracy

The Holy
City, Ria

Capital City, Paneramare

The Kingdom
of Felsen

Berge,
Capital of Beasts

Capital City, Atryle

The Sea of Trees

The
Kingdom
of Ryle

Capital City, Lestein →

The Knight
Kingdom of Lestia

Dragoness Island

Retrobamba

The Kingdom
of Sandora

Kyuray,
The Sandy Capital

The Kingdom
of Egret

New World

I'd informed just about everyone possible about the incoming merging of worlds. I used the world leaders from both worlds, Relisha's guild network, and Silhouette's Black Cats to spread the word and warn the population of any unusual circumstances that could spring up.

God Almighty said nothing huge would happen, but I wanted us to be safe rather than sorry. For that reason, I decided to close off Brunhild's dungeon islands for the appointed day.

I had a lot riding on the pillar spirits and their subordinates, too. They'd be in charge of holding back earthquakes, volcanic eruptions, tsunamis, and other such natural disasters. Thankfully, I had enough advance notice to put these countermeasures in place.

Spirits didn't typically get involved with stopping stuff like natural disasters, but I asked them to lend me their power nonetheless. I was fairly sure they didn't want the world to end anyway, so it was all good.

Thus, all I could do at this point was pray nothing bad would happen.

And, after three days… Dawn broke upon a new world.

I woke up before my smartphone's alarm went off. I'd hardly slept, to be honest. After all, any time after midnight could've been the merger… God Almighty didn't exactly have an exact schedule for when it was happening.

"Good morning."

"Morning… Are you okay, Touya?" Yumina looked a bit concerned. She probably saw the bags under my eyes.

We decided that we'd spend the whole day relaxing with each other, waiting for the event to happen.

Everyone felt uneasy, though. After breakfast, they all gathered in the living room, reading or playing cards together.

I sat down on the couch and browsed news stories on my smartphone, and briefly realized that some kind of emergency broadcast system for everyone's smartphones would be useful. I called Doctor Babylon and told her I wanted to do that, and she said it would be pretty easy if we used the spirits to generate real-time information on natural disasters.

It was a little late to make one before the merge, but I decided to make it for future events. Warnings for tsunamis or wildfires would be incredibly useful.

Just as I ended the call and flicked to the next new story on my smartphone, it happened. A massive rumble rang through the ground. Everything shook ferociously. The initial quake wore off, ultimately giving way to a few small rumblings that persisted in the background.

"It's time…"

"T-Touya…" Sue walked over to me and clung to my side. I knew it would be okay, though. I had the spirits out there mitigating any damage.

"Touya, look at the sky!" Linze yelled out from the balcony. I walked over there with Sue clinging to my leg and looked up. The sky was black, even though it was supposed to be morning. Thick, heavy clouds roamed around the sky above.

"Wh-What's that light up there?"

"It is beautiful, it is. But it feels strange, it does…"

Lu pointed upward at a strange arc of bright light in the sky. Yae stared upward with wide eyes.

"Did the sky split?"

"No, it's an aurora. I don't know if they occur in this world, but it's a kind of natural light phenomenon."

"It's the Aurora Borealis. They're usually localized above the Sea of Trees, but this is my first time seeing them despite my longevity…" Hilde looked uneasy as Leen followed up with a basic explanation. Back on Earth, they were seen in the frozen north, but it seemed to be a bit different here.

We looked up at the sky as the ground continued to rumble, but the rumbling was so faint at this point that it was kind of like being on a weak water bed.

The sky began to change color. It cycled from red, to green, to purple, and so on. Eventually, it faded, and rain began to fall. We went back inside from the balcony.

The rain was fairly light, just a bit of a drizzle. But there was something off about it.

"It's made of light…?" Sakura muttered as she looked upward. The raindrops fell and glittered myriad colors as they pattered to the ground.

The rain didn't pool or form puddles; it simply faded into the ground below as if a sponge was soaking it up. I reached a hand out a window, and even though I felt the sensation of raindrops on my skin, my hand remained dry.

I put a cup out on the balcony, and none of the rain collected inside that either. I had no idea what was going on.

"It's some form of liquid rife with magical energy... Similar to ether liquid, I'd wager... Perhaps the magic in the atmosphere is condensing and falling to the ground..." Leen murmured to herself, clearly curious. I was glad that it wouldn't lead to flooding, but I was certainly unsure about what kind of effects this would have. After all, it could be filling previously magically-barren places with magical energy.

"Oh, the sky's clearing!"

"Ah, so it is... Wait, hold on!"

I looked up in response to Elze's voice, but I noticed something strange as I saw the sun's rays peek through the disappearing clouds.

Two suns were hanging overhead. Both of them were slightly overlapping with each other, too... Like a two-bubble Venn diagram.

Everyone stared up in absolute silence. Slowly, but surely, the two overlapping suns seemed to merge into each other before releasing a flash of light.

The bright flash caused us all to close our eyes tight, and when they opened again, only one sun remained in the skies above.

The gentle earthquakes also ended. I wondered if it was over.

"Open the world map. Project it into the air."

"Understood. Displaying."

The world map wooshed up in front of us, and it revealed what I expected. A map of a whole new world.

If I were to explain things simply, the Reverse World's map was on the left, and the regular world's map was on the right. But there were a few parts of the landscape that had changed.

"Eashen and Egret seem a little further out than they were before... Their equivalents in the Reverse World are pretty far out, too."

"There's a land bridge connecting Panaches and Refreese... I wonder if that'll be okay."

I looked up at the area Yumina pointed out. It seemed like the west border of Refreese now touched the east border of Panaches.

There wasn't a huge overlap of territory, but I was a bit concerned about the people who might've lived there.

I sent the new map data up to Babylon and had the Doc send out an update to everyone. Everyone's phones were probably showing the old maps of their respective worlds.

Doctor Babylon seemed like she'd been expecting the call.

"How's the situation around the world?"

"Nothing to report. No eruptions or tsunamis or anything. The atmosphere's a little sparse right now, but it's within stable levels."

The spirits were doing their best, apparently. I made a mental note to prepare some rewards for them.

After I had the new world maps sent out to everyone, I started scrolling through my contacts list.

I needed to call the Emperor of Refreese, just in case.

"It seems like we're connected, yes... But the other side is a smaller island nation, so I'm not too worried. The Queen of Strain informed me that the King of Panaches is a mild-tempered man, so I'm sure this'll be fine." The Emperor of Refreese seemed to have a fair understanding of the situation, so I was sure he'd be able to get by fine.

I was actually more worried about the positioning of the Curiela Kingdom, which was a nation that was now just a small stretch of water away from both Belfast and Refreese.

I didn't know anything about that kingdom at all, but I'd probably be able to get some info from Strain or Gardio.

I breathed a sigh of relief and felt like things might be okay. However, something rang out, ending that momentary peace. I heard a cracking and splintering sound from the sky above, like a wine glass being ripped apart.

"Wh-What the?!"

"Touya, up there!" Yumina pointed up at the sky.

Something that resembled a shooting star was tumbling to the ground from the east. I used [Long Sense], along with my own divine sight, and managed to grasp its form.

It was a thorn. At least it resembled one. A muddy-gold thorn, some kind of twisted glass barb flying through the air.

It emanated the same filthy divinity that I now associated with the wicked god.

"Run Search! That object's landing site!"

"Searching... Displaying." A little marker fell down on my map. *Shit, it's in Regulus!*

It was just a bit north-east of the capital city in some open plains. I was only thankful that it didn't seem to be near civilization.

But there was no real time for relief, it was clearly something sent by the wicked god. If something like that had fallen into the new world, then I could hardly leave it alone.

"I'll be back in a minute!" It wasn't too far away, so I used [Teleport] to warp there. I didn't want to put the girls in danger, so I went alone. Assuming things were safe there, I'd open up a [Gate] to bring them over after checking it out.

I found myself looking into a gigantic crater. The enormous thorn was lodged inside the crater, squirming as it dug into the ground. Without counting the buried portion, it was at least thirty meters in length.

"What is this?"

I took a few steps forward before I noticed the ground around the thorn changing color, almost like cloth stained by water.

The dull-gold hue began spreading, slowly, through the soil itself.

"The very earth is rotting…"

"Ah…"

A mass of soil nearby rose up and took a feminine form. It was the Earth Spirit. I hadn't summoned her, so she'd used a substitute body from her domain to communicate with me. Her actual body was probably back in the spirit realm.

"This thorn is emitting a venom that corrodes all it comes into contact with. Soon enough, the ground here will disappear from this world."

"Disappear? How?"

"Well, this venom does not truly damage. It eliminates. All the soil it affects will simply have never been, as if vanished from reality itself…"

Huh, so it's not even like melting into magma or something? Stuff just straight-up gets deleted from existence? Man, what the hell is that wicked god sending me annoying things like this for?

"My master, look at it."

The Earth Spirit pointed at the giant barb. It began making chiming sounds as mutated Phrase constructs emerged from inside it. I didn't know whether to be appalled or impressed.

All the mutants from the thorny barb were Lesser Constructs, at least. They brandished their bladed limbs and came charging toward me and the spirit.

I quickly cast [Storage] and pulled out a phrasium hammer, then doubled its weight with [Gravity] and swung it down toward the mutant scum.

They were all crushed along with their cores, leaving their remains to melt into sludge.

I quickly noticed that more and more mutants were coming out of the thorn, and no matter how many I mashed, they didn't seem to be stopping.

Seemed like I needed to handle the disease rather than the symptoms.

I mashed a few more newborn mutants before aiming my hammer at the thorn with a full-powered swing.

I felt the impact when I hit against its surface, and it let out a noise like a gong being impacted.

Cracks began to run up and down the poisonous barb, splintering here and there. It shattered into fragments that then fell to the ground. With the thorn's destruction came the end of the spreading poison, too.

"Damn it. It really shouldn't be so adaptable. This is borderline harassment at this point."

The thorn's fragments began melting into a thick goop, just like the other mutants when they died. I assumed it would fade away into black smoke like the rest of them as well, but I was wrong...

The liquid goop began to condense and solidify until it was a fine golden powder. The powder began to swirl around in the air as if picked up by the wind, filling the surrounding area with a muddy-gold light.

"What the heck?"

"A-Aughghaugh?!"

The Earth Spirit began screaming, keeling over in agony before falling prone to the ground. I had no idea what had just happened. I ran toward her in confusion, crouching down to hear her out.

"H-Hey, you okay?!"

"I-I'm sorry, I... My master, please run from here... It's... It's..."

The earth that had formed her temporary body collapsed back to the ground before she could finish her sentence.

"The hell is this?"

I rose back to my feet, but I was suddenly assaulted by a dizzying sensation. I began keeling over, much like the Earth Spirit just had.

Wh-What's going on here? I can't feel my legs... I can't... Muster strength... I tried to stand up, but I just slumped forward again. I couldn't find the strength. A cold sweat formed on my brow, back, and all the rest of me. My breathing became ragged as my vision blurred. I felt violently ill.

"Ugh... W-Was it that powder...?"

The golden powder still fluttered in the air like a fine mist, almost taunting me. Breathing in any more of the stuff would be really bad news, so I needed to escape.

"[Tele...port]..."

My magic isn't working? No, why? Is the powder causing this as well? What do I do?! I couldn't draw any magic power from inside me at all. I tried again, but nothing happened. I tried to muster my divinity from within me as a last resort, but the moment I felt my apotheosis trigger, my body was wracked with horrible pain. I began vomiting violently, and my entire form lay paralyzed against the ground.

"Bwugh!" I rolled to the side, just narrowly avoiding my own puke. I could look up at the sky at this point, but what I saw made me wish I was dreaming.

"...Th-This can't be happening..." In the western skies, I saw a horrible sight. Dozens of meteors in the sky, each clad in muddy-gold light. They were falling down as a group, each likely the same as the thorn I'd just destroyed. Nausea ran through my body again, and I could do nothing but watch as each thorn descended.

I tried again to move, but it was futile. There was nothing I could do.

I... I can't even keep my eyes open anymore... What do I do...?

"Gwuh!"

"G-Grand Duke!"

I suddenly saw the hazy image of a girl with pinkish hair. *Sakura? Oh... You must've teleported...*

I saw her running toward me, tears in her eyes. It was the last thing I saw before my vision went black.

My eyes felt heavy as I opened them. A familiar ceiling came into view.

I was in my room, in my bed.

"You're awake now, you know?"

"…Hey, Karen."

Karen sat by my bed. There was a mass-produced smartphone in her hands.

I tried to sit up, but my body felt so sluggish I could barely move.

"You should stay laying down in bed, you know? The divine venom only just left your system, so your strength'll take a while to return."

"…I'm sorry, what?"

"It's a type of poison that can kill gods. I didn't really expect the enemy to have that kind of thing at their disposal, you know?" Karen grumbled quietly to herself, arms folded.

Venom… huh? I guess it did feel like I'd been poisoned.

Karen explained that the divine venom was a poison used to kill members of the pantheon. The stronger the divinity of the target, the stronger the effects on the body. Apparently, my divine relatives were extremely concerned that the wicked god had something like that available to it.

That made sense, since the pain only got worse when I activated my apotheosis.

Apparently, Karen had sensed it, but neither she nor the other gods could save me. Human bodies or not, they were still divine. They'd have collapsed on the spot if they came nearby.

Sakura bravely volunteered to rescue me, since she could use teleportation magic. Apparently, her being a beneficiary of divinity meant the poison affected her as well, and she'd slept for a whole day.

"She was out a whole day? Wait, what about me?"

"Three days. It was a really big issue, you know? Everyone was so scared that they barely left your bedside. My little brother sure is a popular guy, you know?"

Three days… I guess everyone was worried about me. I'll have to say sorry later.

"So the venom's gone from my body now?"

"Divine venom only takes effect while you're in contact with it, you know? Now you're out, you'll be fine."

Oh, that's a relief. So as long as I keep away, I'll be fine… Wait. Wait! Didn't I see a bunch of thorns falling to the ground?!

"Display map!"

"Displaying." My smartphone, which was on the side table, responded to my voice. It projected the new world's landmass into the air.

"What…?!"

I was at a loss for words. On the western side of the map, on the Reverse World's side, a portion was missing. Or rather, a portion had basically been cut off from the main continent.

The north and east of Isengard's territory had been completely eaten away, isolating it from the rest of the landmass as a solitary, damaged island.

"This can't be…"

"It was the same thing as the one you destroyed, you know? Just lots of them. They all landed around the Isengard area and the very land itself disappeared."

"So it was those thorns…"

Just as the Earth Spirit warned me, the very earth had been eaten away. The one I'd stopped hadn't managed to take effect, but clearly, it was dire. Water had filled in the gaps left behind.

"But why did they only fall down around Isengard?"

"Smaller ones fell in other areas, you know? But according to Regina, most of them went for this place because something got buried there in the past. She said that the remains or something might have drawn the thorns there, you know?"

Karen pointed to a spot on the map, and it all clicked together. It was the spot where the giant golden tree had appeared a while back. All of that might have been in preparation for this attack; the golden spores it emitted might have acted as some kind of marker directing the missiles...

"So what happened to Isengard?"

"...We don't know, you know? The only thing we do know is that the divine venom is coating the entire landmass."

"The whole thing?!"

"We can't even use our divinity to look over there, you know? The venom creates interference, like TV static." Seemed like the entire country had been corrupted with poison that interfered with divinity. There was nothing we could do. I had wondered why no cities were appearing on the Isengard map, even though I could make out the new shorelines, but it was probably blocking my search magic too.

What do I do? I won't be able to use my teleportation, either... Hell, even if I could I'd probably fall unconscious or die due to the venom anyway.

It'd be easier if I knew a non-divine person with both teleportation and searching magic, but... I didn't exactly know any regular humans with that level of talent.

"It's a bit weird though, you know? Divine venom affects gods no matter what. Even if the wicked god is a mockery with a small amount of divinity, it should be just as affected..."

"I have a theory about that."

Moroha appeared next to Karen as if out of nowhere... My divine relatives always had a habit of doing that.

"I always wondered why the wicked god stayed in the gap between worlds, and why it never actually showed itself. Now I think I get it. It was trying to build an immunity to the divine venom."

"It was?"

"Yeah, I think bit by bit, it was getting used to doses of the stuff. It's a wicked god with a murky divinity to begin with, so it might now have a body capable of withstanding the divine venom."

"...No, I'd say withstanding isn't the right word. I think it imbibed the venom."

Karina walked in from the balcony window. *Hey, c'mon! I know you're a hunter, but couldn't you have used the door like everyone else?!*

"...Imbibe? How do you mean?"

"What do weak animals in the wild do to prevent themselves from being eaten?"

"Huh? I mean, sometimes weak animals form symbiotic relationships with predators... Or they camouflage themselves to hide, or they move around in groups instead. Oh... Now I get it."

"Right. By taking in a toxin that can kill gods, the wicked god has rendered us incapable of hunting it. That was truly a cunning plan on its part, I must say. After all, now gods and those benefiting from their divinity can't go after it."

Poisonous creatures were divided into two sections in the wild. Those that used poison to hunt, and those that used poison to keep themselves from being hunted.

Creatures in the former category were animals like snakes or scorpions. They used their poison to weaken prey, and it was an effective hunting tool.

Creatures in the latter were more like poison dart frogs or pufferfish. They secreted a poison that deterred predators from coming near them.

The wicked god had clearly chosen to immerse itself in divine venom to defend itself. The stronger the divinity, the stronger the effects. But that made me think of something.

"...Does the divine venom work on regular humans?"

"It'd be ineffective. It's completely harmless to anything that isn't a god or those benefiting from a god's divinity. But it can eat its way through magic barriers pretty easily, so even your [Prison] spell couldn't contain it," Moroha quickly replied. If even spells like that wouldn't work, it was clearly formidable. Just as I pondered to myself, two other voices piped up.

"S'plenty lucky that the place with all the venom's an island now. Divine venom's the kinda thing that gets absorbed into the earth an' spoils it. But Isengard's got sea surroundin' it now, which'll dilute the toxins until they ain't active no more. That means it won't spread to the rest've the world."

"But it'sh, hic! Still bad! The divine venom'sh corrupting all that land, hic! We're godsh, sho we can't go there, hic! Sh'like a poison shwamp."

The god of agriculture and the god of alcohol started speaking as they leaned back on a nearby sofa. I hadn't even noticed them enter the room. Still, it seemed like the airborne divine venom would soak into the earth in high concentrations, changing it into a corrupted zone that gods couldn't enter safely…

That kind of reminded me of a famous American comic superhero who was weak to a specific kind of rare material…

"What about the citizens of Isengard?"

"Not much, really. The divine venom has contaminated the island, but obviously, it's not harmful to regular humans. However, it's a dangerous and lawless zone now. Mutants are popping up all over the island and killing indiscriminately. We heard this information from a group of survivors who boarded a boat and arrived on the mainland."

As Moroha spoke, I heard Erik Satie's Gymnopedies being played slowly on a guitar. The music was coming from my closet.

At this point, I wasn't even going to bother thinking about it. The god of music was playing sad music while hiding inside my bedroom closet. So what? It honestly didn't matter at this point.

"You mentioned some of the thorns dropped elsewhere? What happened there?"

"They were smaller, so only a few mutants emerged from them. The adventurer's guild worked with various knight orders to defeat them and bust the thorns. The large ones were all focused on Isengard."

"Is there any divine venom outside of Isengard?"

"The smaller thorns spread some, yes. But it won't harm regular people or animals and should vanish over time. That being said, spirits won't go near those places anymore… So the impacted areas will become small, barren patches of land."

The spirits technically worked as beneficiaries of the gods, so it made sense they'd avoid places that could kill them.

But that also meant that Isengard wouldn't be blessed by any spirits, either... That definitely meant that, over time, Isengard would simply become a barren husk of an island. A place nobody could inhabit at all.

"So, what now? This world's out of God Almighty's domain. It's all up to you now, Touya."

Karina grinned at me. *What now? That should be obvious.*

"I'm gonna beat that wicked god. I won't let it do any more damage than they already have. I'm gonna wipe it out so hard that nobody'll even remember it existed."

Karina and the others glanced at one another, and they shared grins. I was a little bit irritated that they'd all expected me to say something along those lines...

"That's what I like to hear!" Uncle Takeru charged into the room, blasting the door off its hinges as he yelled.

COME ON. WOULD IT KILL A SINGLE ONE OF YOU TO SHOW UP NORMALLY FOR ONCE?!

"We're gonna help you all we can, kiddo! So fight with all your might! I'll carry your body home when it's all over!"

"I-I'm not planning on dying... Also, fix the damn door."

I glared over at Uncle Takeru with an unamused expression. I didn't want him creating bad omens for the future with baseless prattle.

"Touya! You're awake?!"

The girls showed up, having clearly heard all the commotion. Everyone charged toward my bed in a huddle.

Gaaah, Sue! Don't get too close! I reached out and grabbed Sakura by the hand. She had tears in her eyes.

"Thank you. If you hadn't come to get me, then it could've been way worse..."

She slowly shook her head, raising her line of sight to meet mine.

"That's just normal... It's natural for any of us to help you, Grand Duke... We're your wives, and you're our husband. Please count on us more in the future."

...You aren't my wives yet, but I'm happy to hear that from you all the same. I leaned forward and gave Sakura a big hug. As I pulled back, I caught a glimpse of her smile. She was so darn cute!

"...I'm jealous."

"Well, I guess she deserves it this time around. She was laying in bed for a whole day after what she did, so consider it her reward."

Sue started grumbling, so Elze patted her on the head. If that was a reward, I'd be happy to give it out to any of them whenever they wanted...

Still, the divine venom affecting Sakura meant that all my fiancees were in danger. Given that we intended to beat the wicked god, that was a very serious issue.

"So, what do we do about the venom? If everyone in this room can't do anything, then what about our knight order? Will they be affected?"

"That's hard to say for sure, you know? If it's someone completely unrelated to us, then it should be fine... But even by being affiliated with us, they'll have tiny bits of divinity in them. The effects will be lighter, probably... But anyone you're close to can probably be hurt by the venom, too."

Karen grumbled to herself as she folded her arms. *Seriously? Even people just on close terms with me?*

"Romantic partners, friends, family, those you've done good deeds for, and even those who have just benefited from your goodwill... The divine venom will react to that blessing and eat

31

away at anyone who has it. It's probable that every single person in Brunhild could be affected by the venom at this point, given all you've done. Though the divinity would be so small that they'd probably only suffer nausea, rather than death."

This venom was clearly designed to hurt absolutely everything vaguely related to the gods. What a horrible thing to be up against...

It could affect everyone I've ever known... Somehow that makes me uncomfortable. Guess it won't affect people I don't like or people I barely pay attention to, though.

"S-So is there no countermeasure to deploy against a poison like that?" Linze timidly raised her voice, prompting Uncle Kousuke to speak up.

"Nothing in the human world, kiddo. S'possible Touya could do what the wicked god did and take the poison into himself to try and become resistant to it... But if that happened, none of us or his wives-to-be could ever be near him again."

"Nope! Denied! Not allowed!" Sue immediately shot that idea down. I wasn't exactly a fan of that route either.

"We need to think of a way to get around this. And that... wicked god thing? We can't let it do as it wishes." Lu spoke firmly, but I had no real idea where to start. If everyone in Isengard was dead, we could've opted for remotely sinking the entire island, but I had a feeling they wouldn't go down that easy.

"W-Well, I am not sure this is a plan, I am not... But..." Yae turned toward Karen and raised a hand. I wondered what she was thinking.

"This venom. Does it affect machines as well, does it?"

"Machines? I don't think Frame Gears would work against that, you know? Even Touya's [Prison] spell gets eaten away. Even if you put a protective barrier around the cockpit, you'd—"

"Ah, I did not mean Frame Gears, I did not. What about Gollems?"

I stared blankly for a few seconds before realizing what Yae was getting at.

"For example… if there was a Gollem Touya cared about a lot… would it be affected by the venom and shut down, would it?"

"…Nope, it wouldn't. Gollems fall under the tool category, or weapons, I guess… At most, it'd become something like a sacred treasure, but venom wouldn't affect a non-living creature."

Moroha's explanation made sense. Gollems and Frame Gears wouldn't really be affected by the divine venom. If the venom could affect non-living things, then surely my clothing or smartphone would've been affected too. But they weren't.

I saw a sudden ray of light amidst the darkness I'd just experienced. But if it was Gollems we needed more info on, then we'd have to talk to Elluka. I made immediate plans to head her way.

"Hm… So that divine venom affects anyone Touya likes?"

"Seems like we're in trouble too, Elluka. We probably won't die, but I imagine we'll get a bit dizzy."

Doctor Babylon grinned a bit as she spoke. *Ugh… What a pain…*

We obviously couldn't bring up the whole god thing, so we just covered up the story by making out like it was a regular toxin.

It was just a regular old toxin that happened to exclusively hurt anyone I happened to like.

It was annoying to admit, but Doctor Babylon was right. It'd affect her and Elluka as well. If you asked me whether I cared for them or disliked them, I'd obviously have to say I cared for them…

Despite how irritating the little child-bodied twerp in front of me was, she was still a big part of my life.

"So yeah, we can't really do anything about Isengard. We can't even send scouts out there."

"Really? What if we just sent someone from a place other than Brunhild, then? For example, I'm sure the Black Cats could go in on your behalf. They're not really related to you, are they?"

"Oh, I guess that's true."

I kept getting caught up in the idea that I had to be the one to fight the wicked god, but getting others to scout wasn't a bad idea.

"Still, it'll still be dangerous over there. I kind of feel bad asking others to risk themselves…"

"I get how you feel, but still. Anyway, you said that Gollems won't be affected by this venom?"

"I did. That's why I'm here to see if you can make a recon-type spying Gollem. Or if you know any legacy models that can do that." Elluka leaned back, pondering a while. Eventually, she raised two fingers.

"Two issues with that. First, if we sent out a factory-model, or one I make for you… it'll be largely useless without a master. You should know this from your experience already, but non-legacy Gollems aren't really capable of autonomously following complex orders."

That was true enough. The ones back in the Kingdom of Horn had terrible coordination. We needed a spy drone that could actually react on the fly.

"Second. Assuming my first point holds, we'd have no choice but to use a legacy Gollem. But a legacy Gollem with such sophisticated decision-making skills would need to have had several years of operating experience. It would have to be a Gollem with several years spent serving a master. Obviously, any master who has spent that long with their Gollem would have reservations letting us borrow it for a dangerous mission, right?"

"So you're saying no sensible owner would let us do that."

Most legacy Gollems were dormant once excavated. Since it had been so long since their creation, they'd lost the memories of their past as well and effectively became blank slates. They basically learned everything from the beginning with the help of their new masters.

The three Gollems I owned, Ruby, Saph, and Emerl had also gradually learned things over time. They were getting better at autonomous decision-making.

There was no way sending those three to Isengard would be good. They had no strength at all. Even if they were strong, I wouldn't send them if some random guy came up and asked me to.

Hell, I'd even refuse to sell them.

I doubted that Norn or Nia would want to put Noir or Rouge in that kind of situation either.

"What now...?"

"We could always find a legacy Gollem designed to be good at spying, and start teaching it now."

"If we waste time doing that, the enemy could be making their move. We need to be fast in this."

Maybe our only option to win the race would be going slow and steady... Or maybe I could just ask the Black Cats if they had scouts available to go in on my behalf. But if they ended up meeting mutants, they'd need to be as strong as red adventurers to take them out.

"Well... we could also steal a legacy Gollem."

"I'm not so sure about that one."

I wasn't exactly desperate enough to start committing crimes.

"I don't exactly mean stealing from the innocent. There are a lot of legacy Gollems in use by criminals, after all… Most legacies started as stolen goods to begin with, anyway. I'm talking about that kind."

…I guess that'd be kind of okay?

"Hm. I see what you're getting at, Mistress. You're talking about the Death Wings, aren't you?"

Fenrir, who had been laying down on the floor, raised his head and spoke. I wondered what he was talking about.

"The Death Wings are a bandit group that is active in the Allent Theocracy. They've attacked numerous villages, and are quite hard to find. The reason for this is they seem to have a legacy Gollem built for spying and recon. Exactly the kind you need."

"Gotcha. You're saying we gotta take that one?"

I felt a bit bad, but Gollems themselves weren't criminals. I didn't exactly want to use a tool that a bunch of bandits had been using, but I was generally out of options. Plus, taking out such a villainous group would be a good thing.

"I'd be happy if you did this. The Gollems under that group happen to be my siblings."

"Seriously?"

I raised my brow at Fenrir, who dutifully wagged his tail.

"They're called Anubis and Bastet. They're not exactly from the same line as Fenrir, they're just from the product line that succeeded him. You could consider Fenrir to be their older brother in that regard."

If they were the same as Fenrir, I wondered if that made them animal-based models as well. If they were animal-looking, then that'd be good for surveillance… But I had reservations about the effectiveness of a wolf-shaped drone if they were extremely similar to Fenrir.

Honestly, things probably would've been easier if Fenrir went to Isengard for us.

But… Elluka wasn't a member of Brunhild's forces, she was tentatively a guest of ours. I wasn't shameless enough to ask a guest for help.

Thus, it was settled. We had to steal those legacies from the bandits.

"But where are these guys? A group of outlaws would obviously be hiding away from the law… And I don't know enough to use my search spell…"

"Snakes slither with snakes. Thieves tend to know each other, right? Don't we have someone nearby who fits that description?"

"Ah…"

I knew who Doctor Babylon was referring to immediately. And so, I set off to speak to Nia and the others.

"The Death Wings, eh? We've never met with them directly, but we've heard the stories. They're scumbags who raid villages… They even kill all the men they can find, then sell off the women and children as slaves."

"While it's true they're thieves like us, their philosophy is based differently. We don't have any direct connections, but we may be able to tell you where their hideout is." I was in the Silver Moon, talking with Nia and Est. The two of them pointed up toward the map I was projecting.

It was a location not too far from the Allent Theocracy, a desert area near Dauburn, Land of Fire.

"I've heard stories their base is around here. They attack all over, but obviously, they'd need to keep their loot in one place. It's probably here, on account of the nearby oasis." Nia jabbed a finger toward a sprawling oasis in the desert.

"Do the Death Wings have an emblem or anything I could use to identify them?"

"I've heard their members have tattoos of a winged reaper on their shoulders." *Well, that's simple enough.*

"Run search. People with winged grim reaper tattoos on their shoulders."

"Searching… Search complete. Displaying." A few markers fell down on the map. Some were spread out, but there was a particular area with a higher density than usual.

"…Your magic is certainly something else. If anyone else had it, I'm sure they could wipe out thieving bands as a concept…"

"This magic isn't exactly unstoppable. It's just that the Reverse World's magic is too far behind. You don't have countermeasures for it, not widespread ones at least. Now the two worlds are connected and swapping information, I'm sure you'll bridge that gap in no time." People who weren't in the know probably had no idea about the newly-merged world yet.

I was sure that the two halves of the new whole would have plenty of arguments with each other… It was imperative that I set up a meeting between all the leaders, while also keeping an eye on Isengard.

Either way, it seemed like this bandit group had done all manner of awful deeds, so I had no qualms about going in hard on them. I'd hand them over to the knight order without a second glance.

Heheh... Fools, I'm gonna trash your home and make off with your precious machinery...

...No, Touya. Stop! That's exactly how an actual bandit would think!

The Death Wings had their base set up in a crumbling ruin by the oasis.

"B-Bastard! Who are ya, huh?! You with the Theocracy?!"

"Nope. But sort of, I guess. I'm here to round you up, either way." There was one man left standing amidst a sea of unconscious criminals. Obviously I was responsible.

This guy was clearly the leader. His leather armor was of a higher grade than the others, and he also wore a fancy cape.

It had taken me but a few moments to isolate the Gollems I was after with **[Prison]**. Then I just used **[Storage]** to stash them. Anubis looked like a black dog, and Bastet looked like a black cat.

If they'd been using those Gollems to spy, then there was no wonder they'd always managed to stay one step ahead of the authorities.

The Gollems had attacked me in tandem and shown that they were clearly suited to assassination as well.

"Y-You here to claim our bounty, then?! H-Hey, I can give you more gold than the Theocracy's offerin'! No lie, friend! I got more gold here than... Gaugh!" I shot a paralyzing bullet into the leader's face. I didn't like that sleazy smile on his face.

"Thanks, but no thanks. I'll be taking your money and donating it to the needy. Hope you can rest well in prison knowing your money's going to those who can actually make use of it." I gathered up the bandits and put them in a big pile, then I warped them straight to the Allent Theocracy's authorities, much like how I dealt with the thugs back in Horn.

If I went there formally I'd be able to claim their bounties, but I was supposed to be doing this covertly and I didn't care for the paperwork.

The idea of a world leader heading to wipe out a criminal group just because he wanted Gollems was a little much... Plus, I didn't want to upstage the good people of Allent.

I found the treasures they'd been hoarding and threw them all into [Storage]. I'd use this to give back to the poor and the people they'd hurt. *Man, I know most of this is going to orphanages and stuff, but there's a lot of treasure here... Maybe beating bandits is more profitable than I expected.*

I considered that bandit-crushing could be a good training activity for the Brunhild knight order. We could also incorporate any appropriated assets into the monthly pay bonuses, while making the world just a little bit safer. It would probably be harder to track down bandits that didn't have conveniently-identifiable shoulder tattoos, though.

I finished gathering up the treasure and headed back out of the ruins. The glare of the sun shone directly into my eyes.

Ugh... Why's the desert always so hot... Wait... Is that something in the distance? Something falling this way...? Wh- Huh?!

I jumped to the side, just narrowly avoiding the scythe. One of the stone pillars by the ruin's entrance was cleaved diagonally, sliding down to the sands below.

"Beep..." The kicked-up sand around me dispersed, and what I saw in front of me was a small purple Gollem with a huge scythe in its hands. It was the purple crown, Fanatic Viola. That could only mean one thing... "Oh my, oh me... Mommy Luna was sooo sad about all these bandits being gone... But it looks like I'm lucky after all. Who would've thought I'd meet you here, Tou? Ah... The red string of fate really connects us, doesn't it? So tightly wound around our necks... I'd love to pull it even tighter!" The voice came from the woman standing atop a nearby pillar. She was holding a parasol in her hand.

She had amethyst hair, a complexion like a doll, gothic clothing and a multi-layered skirt. Her eyes were two deep pools of insanity, staring intently at me from behind her glasses.

Luna Trieste. The master of the purple crown... The Frenzied Mistress...

"...What are you doing here?"

"Don't be so mean, Tou! Isn't that obvious? I came here to mulch those naughty bandits to pulpy paste. I found a village that had every last person all dead and leaking goopy guts... So I thought I'd come here to see if the nasty boys wanted to play with me too. But now you're here, Tou! I don't have to worry anymore!" Luna jumped from the pillar to the sands beneath her and discarded her parasol.

Or at least, she only discarded the shade part of it. *Wh... She was hiding a sword under there?!* She charged at me, attacking me with the sword and almost treating it like a whip. She was fast. Not quite as adept as Yae or Hilde, but still remarkably impressive.

I dodged each blow, just narrowly. But they kept on coming.

"Ahahaha! Amaaazing! Beautiful! So lovely! But this isn't fun if I'm the only one doing it! You gotta fight back, Tou! You need to gouge me, please! Thrust inside, dig around... Punch me, pierce me, kick me and kill me!"

"Sorry, lady. That's not my kink. **[Prison]**!"

"Ah?!" I generated an invisible barrier around Luna, trapping her inside.

"Oh my oh me! What's this? Is this your magic, Tou?"

"It's a sealing spell called **[Prison]**. Those walls won't break unless I want them to, so you better give up now."

"Violaaa... Can you give it a try, sweetie?"

"Beep." The purple Gollem swung its scythe against the walls, but it was fruitless. Since I'd mixed a small portion of my own divinity into the barrier, there was no way they could break out.

Viola's weapon was repelled again. There was no point in them trying a thing.

"Ahaha, wowie! Okay, Viola! You step aside, okay? I'm gonna give it my best shot, promise!"

"I told you, you don't have a chance here. Now be good and... Wh... What..." Luna tossed away her sword, and I could only stare in horror as her right arm began oozing a muddy-gold metallic substance. It began coating her arm, sliding all the way up to her elbow and hardening until her forearm had become a golden spear.

"Here goes nothing! Teehee!" Luna thrust out her right arm, and I heard a crack. In a few seconds, the cracking spread. The **[Prison]** had completely collapsed.

"I-It broke! Wowie zowie! That's amazing! Ahahaha, oh... It hurts! It hurts so bad! Whenever I use this power it's like my body's getting sliced and diced and mulched and crushed! Ohh... It hurts so bad I might just squirt... Aah... Holding back is way too hard, you know?" *You have to be kidding me...*

I stared, unable to believe what I was seeing. Muddy-gold metallic fragments started sprouting out of Luna's body. She looked uncomfortably similar to the Dominant Construct Phrase.

But worse still was the fact that I unmistakably felt the divinity of the wicked god emanating from her insides.

What the hell happened to her?

She has Phrase mutant qualities… She has wicked divinity in her… How?

"You…"

"Hm? You mean this? I got attacked by some mean golden monster! It kept growing back no matter how many times I smashed and cut at it! It was just like me, kind of! We kept attacking and cutting each other… And then this happened! We kind of mixed together, don't really know how! Ahaha!"

"What?!" *Seriously? Did the purple crown's regeneration ability react to the mutant's regeneration and overpower it or something? I don't understand…*

"I get a little messier and horrible when I use this power, though… But it should be okay if I'm fighting you, Tou!"

"Are you serving the wicked god now, or something?"

"Serving the wicked what now? Huh?" Luna looked legitimately confused. Seemed like she hadn't been corrupted by the mutants, this was just a really horrible coincidence.

"That power comes from a wicked god, a corrupt member of the divine. You should expel it from your body, bad things'll happen."

"No way! I wanna use this power to play with you more, Tou! Just like this!!" The golden spear extended toward me like a certain famous pole weapon. I quickly drew Brunhild and parried the attack away.

But the spear changed its course as it extended, aiming toward me from behind. I dodged to the side, and the tip of her weapon pierced the ground.

"Aw gosh… I'm not good at handling my wiggly stabby arm yet…" The motion she'd used reminded me of the attacks used by Phrase and their mutant variants. I was not at all happy that an absolute maniac like Luna had gotten her hands on this kind of power.

As I quietly cursed fate, Viola approached me with its scythe.

I blocked the blow using Brunhild, letting the blade of its weapon sink into the ground. Viola turned and moved to make another attack, so I aimed a magic spell toward its feet.

"[Slip]!"

"Beep?!" Viola fell face-first into the ground.

"Ahahaha! Viola, you look so dumb!" I ignored Luna, who decided now was an appropriate time to start pointing and laughing at her own Gollem, and I pulled a phrasium broadsword out of my **[Storage]**.

I raised it above my head, imbued it with **[Gravity]** to increase the weight, and brought it crashing down on the prone Gollem.

The impact created shockwaves along the ground.

Viola was left in a hideous state, crushed and hacked in half from head to waist. It wouldn't be able to regenerate that kind of damage. Not easily, at least.

In truth, I felt pretty bad about it. Viola looked strikingly similar to the red crown, Rouge, so it gave me cause for brief hesitation.

Plus, even if they were just machines, it's not like I enjoyed causing damage to things that were arguably conscious.

"Hiyaah! Take this! Viola's-Revenge-Attack!"

"What?!" Luna had changed her right arm into a broadsword, likely to fight on even grounds with me.

Despite its impressive size, Luna swung it around as if it weighed nothing, probably because it was part of her body. She came charging toward me with a horizontal strike.

"**[Shield]!**" I realized my mistake far too late. Even if it was faint, that sword-arm of hers had divinity inside it. An ordinary **[Shield]** spell couldn't hope to do a thing.

"Gah!" My spell was shattered, and I was sent flying into a nearby wall.

I should've used my head... Would've been smarter to parry it with a weapon than try to block it with magic.

Luna leaped over toward me as I tried to get back up. She held me down with her knees, straddling me until she was fully mounting my body.

I looked up at her eyes, which had a devious fire burning inside them.

"Caught you... Ehehe... You're all mine now. You know, Tou... Whenever I fight you, my body gets all heated up... I fluster and burn so very easily... Is this love or something? It's love, right? Oho... Ehe... I have a great idea."

"Huh?! Wh- Hey!" Luna, still firmly mounting my body, began undoing the ribbon binding her clothes. She started to unbutton her top, bit by bit. I could see the black lace of her bra peeking out...

"Wh-What the hell are you doing?!"

"Don't worry, you'll be fine. I don't think it hurts for boys on the first time... But it might hurt for the girl... Maybe even a lot! I want it to hurt a lot..."

"The hell are you talking about?!" Luna looked down at me with a manic smile on her face. Her breathing grew ragged. She licked her lips in an alluring manner as she glared down at me like a predator.

Wh-What the hell?! I found myself in a panic, and then my arms were suddenly seized. I looked up and saw the one grabbing me was a small, purple being.

It was the Gollem I'd obliterated earlier, Viola.

"Wait… It could regenerate even after being trashed that hard?!"

"You thought something like that could kill Viola? Ehehe. Viola regenerates faster than me because Viola can't feel pain, silly!" *But I trashed the G-Cube and the Q-Crystal… What gives?!* I suddenly heard the sound of something falling to the ground, so I looked back at Luna. It was her clothing. She was now straddling me, fully naked, her form backlit by the rising sun.

"AUUUUUUGH?!" My entire body stiffened up from the shock. No other reason. Just shock. Luna's smile had turned lascivious, and her heavy breathing caused her glasses to fog up. The hot sun bore down on her naked body, glistening with fresh sweat.

"Wh-Wh-What the hell is this?! Hold on. What are you even doing?! Stop!"

"Mmf… Don't struggle, it'll feel really good soon…" Luna opened up my shirt and lowered her naked body down to straddle my bare tummy. My arms were well and truly restrained thanks to Viola, and I had nowhere to run. Given that Luna wasn't wearing anything, that meant I was making direct contact with her… Well… That…

"[T-T-T-Teleport]!"

"Whuh?" I instinctively warped away in order to escape. I hadn't even set a target coordinate. I just needed to get the hell out. I ended up rolling on the ground about ten meters away.

That was… Disturbing. I can't even count how many ways that was disturbing…

"Naughty… You're surprisingly meek, Tou. It's cute."

"Quit it!" *I can't handle this. This is way too much for me. This girl is basically my natural predator. If she catches me again, I'm done for. That's why I'm gonna run away! I've already dealt with everything here anyway!* "Well, see ya!"

"Ah, wai-..." I didn't hear the end of Luna's complaints. I'd immediately warped myself to the Theocracy's capital.

I'd planned on warping to a back alley, but I was still thrown off by the incident. I ended up on a rooftop.

I lay back on the roof, calming myself down as I listened to the hustle and bustle of people going about their lives. I could hear a lot of kids and raised voices from some gruff-sounding guys.

"...That was horrible." I felt like a frog cornered by a snake. My heart was beating rapidly. I was just glad I managed to escape before having something important taken from me...

I was parched, so I took out some fruity water from [**Storage**] and gulped it down.

Whew... That hits the spot. At least I can think straight now.

I-I think I'm gonna go home. I did what I needed to do. I'll have Elluka tune up those Gollems, but who should be their master?

It's probably fine if Elluka takes them on, since they're from the same production line as Fenrir. Fenrir should be pretty happy for the company, too.

I was about to head back to Babylon when I remembered the treasure I'd taken from the bandits.

Oh yeah, since I'm in the capital I might as well see about donating to orphanages or whatever.

"Let's see... The closest orphanage. Oh, it's right here." I ran a search for orphanages and a marker fell down right on my current location. I was apparently on the roof of one.

That explains why I've been hearing kids. Explains those gruff guys, too.

Wait... Gruff guys? I glanced down from the roof.

I saw three thuggish men yelling at a woman; a group of children cowered behind her.

"The deadline's tomorrow, lady! Might as well pack your shit and get outta here. Take the brats already!"

"P-Please... Think of the children. If we're evicted, just where can they go?"

"Like I give a shit! Send 'em to the slums or something!" I didn't know the details but it was clear these people were in some trouble.

These guys sure look like assholes... Oh? What's this? A carriage drawn by black Gollems pulled up in front of the orphanage. A man slowly emerged from inside the ornate vehicle.

"Boss!"

"You guys're taking way too long here. It's just some shitty kids, isn't it? Kick 'em out already." The man referred to as their boss took a cigar out and placed it into his mouth. One of the thugs hurriedly lit it for him.

He was a chubby man, clearly over thirty. He wore a Chinese-style changshan gown. He had a balding head and some unnecessarily gaudy gold glasses on his face. His whole image was tacky. He also had a wispy mustache that made him look a bit like a catfish... But that wasn't the most important thing here... I'd seen this guy somewhere before. He felt familiar, at least. "M-Mister Zabbit, we'll get your money! Please have mercy!" The older woman, likely the orphanage owner, pleaded in front of him. He kicked at her and spat at the ground in disgust.

Zabbit… Zabbit? "Don't cha touch me with them filthy paws, granny. Don't ya get it? This is Papillon's turf now, dig? Get the hell outta here, and take those brats with-"

"OH! THAT'S WHERE I KNOW YOU FROM!" I heard the word Papillon and it all came together. Ideally, I'd have never heard from this asshole again, but now I clearly remembered him.

He looked up toward my sudden exclamation, and sheer fear washed over his face.

Zabbit Grandt. He was one of the leaders of Papillon… Although technically he was now the sole leader. I'd only met him briefly, so it was fair to say he hadn't left a strong impression.

Papillon was the underground organization that Silhouette and the other Black Cats used to belong to.

Zabbit constantly caused Silhouette and her brothels grief because he wanted control of her information network.

In the end, I cast a curse on the moron in order to make him cool off.

It was a curse that would slowly paralyze him if he or his subordinates harassed Silhouette any more.

Zabbit took Papillon and fled, though I hadn't expected him to flee all the way to a neighboring country.

The organization certainly looked sloppier than it used to. From what I'd heard, though, several other key members left when Silhouette did.

I hopped down from the rooftop, landing in front of Zabbit and his lackeys.

His face paled, but he still managed to open his mouth and yell at me.

"Wh-What the hell are you doing here, huh?!"

"Just passing through. Call it a lucky coincidence. You still causing trouble, huh? Want me to put a nastier curse on you?"

"Eek!" Zabbit turned and ran from me. It seemed like his legs weren't paralyzed, at least.

"[Slip]!"

"Bwroagh!" He fell forward and smashed his face against the sidewalk.

"You bastard!"

"What'd you do to our boss, huh?!"

"Shut it. I'm not in the mood to mess around today. **[Gravity]**."

The three goons yelled out as I made them fall to the ground under their own body weight.

"Hey."

"Eep... Y-Yes?!"

"How much does this orphanage owe you, exactly?"

"Th-Three platinum coins! I-I-It's a proper arrangement, honest! I have paperwork!" He took out a document from his breast pocket. It actually looked legit. Three platinum coins were around three million yen, if I recalled properly. According to the deed they had to pay up or surrender their property to Papillon.

"Well, whatever. I was planning on donating money to the orphanage anyway. Here. Three platinum."

"What?" I casually passed three platinum coins over to Zabbit. Knowing that greedy bastard, he was hoping to claim the land with shady interest tactics. Too bad for him. He'd take the money and have to like it.

"All good, right?"

"Huh? Wait, but..."

"Boy, you must really want another curse put on you, huh."

"Nooooo!" I was only making a joke, but it scared Zabbit so much that he leaped to his feet and ran full pelt toward his Gollem carriage.

"B-Boss?!" I released the weight magic on his three henchmen, and they chased after him at incredible speeds.

"U-Uhm… Who are you?" The orphanage owner nervously spoke to me.

I picked up the loan deed that Zabbit had left behind, and I burned it to cinders.

"Just a traveler. I was told to donate money to the local orphanages. I'll be giving some to the other orphanages too, so don't worry yourself."

"D-Donate? But that's so much!"

"I don't know the exact details, I'm just doing this thanks to an anonymous benefactor. I've used up three platinum coins to square your debt, but I hope this amount will help you run the place." I made up a convenient excuse as I passed seven platinum coins to the woman.

There were five other orphanages in the city of Allen.

I decided to give ten platinum coins to all of them. The money the bandits had didn't quite make up that amount, but the valuables they'd been hoarding would likely cover the difference.

The orphanage owner bowed her head to me as I passed out snacks to all the kids.

Alright, time to hit the other orphanages, then back to Babylon.

I gotta take a break today, honestly. I don't feel like doing anything after all this crap. I need to clear my head, get some real rest and relaxation.

I shook my head from side to side, desperately trying to erase the naked form that had been scorched into my mind by the burning sun. I sighed, opening up a **[Gate]** to the next orphanage.

"We are tasked with investigating the nation of Isengard?"

"That's right, yeah. Don't go too far, though. You need to prioritize your safety over anything else." The black cat Gollem, Bastet, nodded its head. The black dog Gollem, Anubis, wagged its tail dutifully.

They were just as good as Fenrir when it came to communication.

"Leave it to me, boss-man! I'll blast them all away! Woof, woof!" I was a little worried about the dog, honestly. Fenrir seemed to notice that and thwacked his little sibling on the head.

"Owie! What's that for, bro?"

"You aren't meant to fight anyone. Sneak around and get some information. That's your priority here, got it?"

"Indeed. Our esteemed brother is right. Please do not go dragging me down." Apparently, Fenrir was the older sibling, Bastet was the middle sibling, and Anubis was the youngest sibling. Anubis was a little larger in size than Bastet, though.

"C'mon sis! I won't drag us down. You think I'm that dumb?"

"I really do."

"Hey, don't say that! Dogs are smart!" *...I think there are a lot of dumb dogs out there... And you're a Gollem, anyway!*

Fenrir and his siblings were certainly well-developed in terms of personality, though.

I wondered if their Q-Crystals were of a higher grade than usual.

"If you're in danger, then run away at once. You're equipped with the means to do so for a reason." Elluka gently pet Bastet on the head as she spoke.

I'd gotten the two Gollems to prevent her from sending her beloved Fenrir out to a dangerous place but ended up making her form a bond with the replacements anyway. Talk about counterintuitive.

As an apology for the risk, I'd granted several powers to the Gollems.

I'd enchanted them with [Storage], [Accel], [Shield], [Fly], and [Invisible] on their bodies, along with [Paralyze] and [Gravity] for their claws. There was no way they could be harmed by regular humans or Gollems anymore.

Apparently keeping in wireless communication with them would be easy, too.

They weren't living beings, so the divine venom didn't have any effect on them.

It was a deadly poison to me and anyone affiliated with me, so we'd have to send them off from a nearby country.

I opened a [Gate] and took them to the western shores of Gardio, facing Isengard.

I tried to use my divine sight to look over at the faraway island, but everything was obscured by a murky golden mist.

People without any divinity wouldn't be able to see it, and it wouldn't have any effect on them, but there was no doubt I was seeing traces of the venom in the air.

"Don't forget to report in often. You'll be scouting for a month. Return here after a month even if you haven't gathered all the info you wanted to gather. If you request a pickup, we'll send someone immediately."

"Understood!"

"Yessir!" I had a feeling Bastet would be more than fine, but I was still a touch worried about Anubis.

"Hey, Anubis. Remember to keep quiet over there, okay?"

"Huh? What for? Bwah!" Anubis found himself slapped across the snout by his sister.

"You dummy! A talking dog would totally stand out!"

"Ohh, that makes sense. Gotcha, no problem! Woofity woof!"

"...Bastet. I'll be counting on you to keep him under control."

"I'll make good use of him. Idiot or not."

"Y-You two are being a bit mean!" Bastet hopped up on to her silly brother's back.

They then promptly floated away using [**Fly**].

"Take care out there."

"Will do! Look after our master!"

"Yup, we're off!" Anubis activated [**Accel**] and blasted away across the surface of the water at the speed of sound. They kicked up a hell of a lot of water in their wake...

Didn't I just say not to stand out?! I really hope nobody's looking in this direction.

After a short time I noticed Anubis vanish into thin air, probably thanks to [**Invisible**]. I had a feeling it was Bastet's call, rather than his.

Wonder if they'll be okay...

Still, I had no choice but to trust in them. I had other things I needed to do.

"It's a pleasure to meet you. I'm Mochizuki Touya, Grand Duke of Brunhild."

"The pleasure is all mine. I'm the King of Panaches, Rabert Tell Panaches. I welcome you to my humble kingdom." A good-natured old man with a white beard smiled over toward me.

He was definitely over seventy, but he had the handshake strength of a man much younger.

I was at the Panaches Kingdom's royal castle.

I'd been sent over to help them prepare for their meeting with Refreese, which was set for a few days later.

Refreese and Panaches were the only two countries to become directly connected by land after the worlds merged.

The northwestern border of Refreese was now fused with the eastern region of Panaches.

The overlapping land was small, a bit bigger than Brunhild, and was currently uninhabited. I didn't think it'd cause many issues.

But it was still something the two countries needed to discuss, so the Emperor of Refreese was set to visit Panaches for a formal meeting.

He'd be coming over thanks to my teleportation, of course. Me visiting Panaches in advance would also help me establish a good area to **[Gate]** him in later on.

I had Kohaku with me, along with our knight order's vice-commander Nikola. There were a few knights in tow, as well. It was really just a formality, though.

"I heard about you from my boy, Robert. He told me you rode a massive Gollem, but despite your ferocious strength, you have a humble disposition. I've also heard you fly around the world for the sake of peace and prosperity, and that you have an honorable and kind nature." ...*Ahaha, I'm sounding almost like a saint here.*

I looked toward the prince. He was standing there in his pumpkin pants, next to his light-blue Gollem.

"That's right, father! Mister Mochizuki Touya is a stellar man, a great man! He's a great friend as well! A wise and noble man with an open mind! He's nothing but righteous!"

"…Don't mention it, Prince Robert."

Come on, dude… I know you don't mean anything bad, but you're kind of raising expectations a little high here. Also, when were we friends?

Norn and Nia definitely said it before, but he's a troublesome prince indeed. The fact that he's not actually a bad person makes this extra annoying to deal with.

The blue crown, Blau, was bowing profusely in my direction. It was just about the only thing stopping me from accidentally muttering about how tone-deaf this guy was.

Still, even if I made a comment, I had my doubts he'd even register it.

I passed on a mass-produced smartphone to the king as I discussed the upcoming Refreese visit with him.

The Reverse World nations with smartphones were… Primula, Triharan, Strain, and Gardio.

Silhouette of the Black Cats also had one, though.

I passed it over thinking it'd be better to have more countries in touch, but Panaches had been an island nation beforehand so it probably didn't have much in the way of diplomatic ties. Still, since it was now connected to the mainland through Refreese, I had a feeling that things would change.

After I finished my meeting, Prince Robert came asking me for a smartphone. I was honestly conflicted about whether to give him one or not.

He kind of seemed like the guy who'd send you a ton of texts in quick succession.

Robert had the ability of spatial manipulation thanks to Blau's power. He could teleport just like me, but the compensation for this power resulted in him needing to sleep after using it.

I couldn't blame his dad for being so worried about him. It seemed like the king thought it would be good if his son had a smartphone, so he could keep in touch with his son.

Prince Robert was born when his father was quite old, so the king ended up doting on him and coddling him a lot.

Despite that, the prince didn't grow up to be a selfish or stupid person, just kind of an annoying one. It was clear that he was a good son, and that the king was a good dad.

Given all that information, I had no choice but to accept.

"Thank you so much! We can contact each other whenever now, can't we?"

"Only text if it's not super urgent, and I'd prefer it if you kept those texts concise." I briefly considered giving him Norn and Nia's numbers so he could hassle them rather than me, but I had the mental image of them beating me up for it, so I decided not to.

"Oh, actually..." There was something on my mind, so I turned to the blue Gollem by my side.

"Blau. I have a question, if that's okay."

"Query? Acceptable. State intent."

"Do you know about the white crown?"

"White. You refer to Albus?"

It knows the white crown... I didn't expect a lead at all.

"You have memories of it?"

"This unit's slumber did not last long post-war. This unit still contains several pre-war memories." Blau had been passed down in the Panaches royal family since before the royalty even existed.

It hadn't slept for as long as the other crowns, and thus had some memories of the early days.

Click.

"What can the white crown do, exactly? Is it a restorative ability? The kind that could patch up a barrier?" The two worlds had become one, so I had no doubts the boundary of the new world was under considerable strain.

If the barrier was broken completely, then this world would have no means of defense against external invaders.

The phrase… Or rather, the wicked god's army, was basically like that. And I had no doubt there were other threats in the cosmos, too.

"This unit cannot discuss crown Gollem skills freely. The meister, our manufacturer, has hardcoded such limitations into us." *Hrmph. Guess that makes sense. If they could discuss those things freely, then stuff like weaknesses would be easier to find out. The meister guy, Chrom Ranchesse if I recall correctly… Guess he installed that as a security measure.*

"The white crown, Albus, is a special model. It is designed as one of a pair, complementing the black crown, Noir. It is the ultimate folly, one that will bring all reality to naught." *Well, that's a little ominous. Kind of makes it sound like a doomsday weapon. I thought it'd be like a white mage with healing abilities or something… But that sounds kinda dangerous.*

Click.

"Do you know where the white crown could be?"

"Negative. This unit had believed it to be located with the black crown." *Maybe I should go talk to Elluka about this, there might be some clues wherever Noir was unearthed.*

Click.

"…Do you need to keep taking photos?"

"This is amazing! I have captured the image of you and Blau on this tiny device!"

"Ask for permission before taking photos, man. You gotta have proper manners."

"Oh, I see! Very well! May I take another?"

"No." I curtly declined the prince, who was completely absorbed in his camera app. Despite his appearance, he was actually pretty smart. He only glanced at the manual a bit and immediately knew how his phone worked.

I had a feeling he'd probably start mailing me photos or selfies, so I told him he'd be better off sending those to his poor old dad.

After a little while, the prince started to talk in a more serious tone.

"Actually, Touya. There's something I wish to ask of you."

"...I'll hear you out, at least. But I might not be able to do anything, depends on what you want." *If you ask me to get a selfie with you so you can set it as your wallpaper, then I'll punch you in the teeth. I know you have no grasp of personal space.*

"My fiancee lives in the Kingdom of Strain. I wondered if you could give her one of these phones."

"In Strain? Oh yeah, I think I remember the queen mentioning something like that..." *Her niece, I think... It's not like I don't trust her, she's part of a royal family I have a good relationship with, but I've never met her before.*

Then again, it's not like I can't just confiscate the phone if it's misused. The Touya giveth and the Touya taketh away.

The prince explained that whenever he used Blau's ability to visit Strain, he often had to sleep for a full day as the trade-off, so he didn't get to speak with his fiancee much. That certainly sounded rough.

I'd already given a phone to the Queen of Strain, and Princess Berlietta. One more member of their royal household couldn't hurt.

"We can hand it over ourselves. I'll open up a **[Gate]** to Strain's castle."

"Wonderful! You truly are a wonderful best friend, Touya! Now I can introduce you to Ceres as well! Huzzah!" *So she's called Ceres, huh. Also, wait. When did I become this guy's best friend? It's true I don't have a lot of male friends my age, but still...*

Man, with Ende and this guy, most of my guy-friends are kinda... Weirdos. This might end up being pretty exhausting.

I shrugged a bit before opening up a **[Gate]** to Strain. I certainly hoped Robert was appreciative.

"There's a Dragon in Lestia?"

"Yes, it appeared in a frontier town named Groose. There's been quite a lot of damage so far, unfortunately. It seems to be a formidable creature."

I was training with Hilde a bit when I received a call from her brother, Reinhard. It seemed there'd been a Dragon attack.

"Is it a quadruped?"

"It is. It's a four-legged, Gold-Copper Dragon, as far as I'm aware."

"I wonder if it's a vagrant... I have an understanding with the Dragons, after all." Dragons were a species of monster I could call upon with Luli's power, but I couldn't control certain subspecies like Wyverns.

I thought maybe it was a Wyvern that had attacked Lestia, but it seemed like it wasn't the case.

That was why I assumed it was a vagrant Dragon.

Vagrant Dragons were the lone wolves of the Dragon world. Except... They were Dragons, not wolves. Hopefully that made sense.

They were Dragons that acted according to their own whims, never heeding the advice of their elders. They freely attacked whatever they pleased, even if I'd made a general law to keep away from humans. Seemed like they couldn't control their tempers.

It wouldn't have been a big deal, but it seemed like the other Dragons didn't take it upon themselves to stop the vagrants, so there was always a risk of them harming towns.

The only solution was to quickly take them out whenever I heard about them.

"Got it, then. Want me to kill it for you?"

"Ah, well… If you don't mind, I'd like to kill it with Lestian knights. It's rather dishonorable to always rely on foreign intervention. If you could tell me where it is located, I should be able to handle the rest."

Oh, huh. I guess I didn't really consider the social shame aspect of meddling in people's stuff.

"Hold on a second then, uhh… Run search. Gold-Copper Dragon."

"Searching… Search complete."

I looked at the map, and one of the hits was right on the border of Lestia. That was probably the one we were after.

I used my phone to screenshot the map and then sent it to Reinhard via text.

"You have my thanks. I'll be in touch."

The call was promptly cut off. I wondered if he'd be fine, though… I heard Dragons with reddish coloration were extremely high-tier. Even the Ancient Dragon guarding the sanctuary in the Sea of Trees was red.

"What did my brother want?"

Hilde seemed anxious to know what the call had been about. I wasn't too surprised she was worried. Her brother and I had been discussing a Dragon of all things.

I told Hilde what Reinhard had told me.

"Ah, a Dragon... My brother has long hoped for such an event."

"He's been hoping for it? Why?"

"Our grandfather is a Gold adventurer, as you know. He also has the Dragonslayer title in the guild. And when our father was young, he defeated a Griffon and gained the title of Griffon Killer. My brother always talks about this kind of thing."

Oh, makes sense. I guess since he's the king now, he feels inadequate compared to his predecessors.

The Dragonslayer title was awarded to people by the guild if they killed a Dragon in a party of five or less.

Of course, that was just a guild formality. You could kill a Dragon outside of the guild and still be recognized if you had witnesses.

Though, obviously, if you wanted the formal title, you'd need to bring proof, and if you brought it down with an army, then you obviously wouldn't qualify.

If Reinhard took down this Dragon alone or with a small unit, he could get the same title that his predecessor Galen once earned.

"But still... I can't help but worry. My brother excels at fighting other people, but I'm not so sure if he's as disciplined against monsters. I hope he'll be alright..." I didn't really think that the king would go down so easily, but I could also understand her fears.

Hilde was worried about her older brother. If something happened to Reinhard, then Lestia would be in great trouble. But I still thought it would be rude or unreasonable to butt in on such a personal fight to him.

"...Wanna go spy on him?"

"Ah, yes!"

Hilde smiled. Thus, we headed off to covertly peek at the fight between the Lestian knights and the Dragon.

Three days later, the Lestian knights arrived at the mountainside. The Dragon had claimed the area as its home.

I informed Hilde, and we used [**Gate**] to get to Mt. Parute, at the southern Lestian border. We hid away from their encampment and sent out Kougyoku to keep an eye on them.

"Looks like they're fine for now."

Kougyoku's vision was transmitted through Hilde's smartphone screen, sending her a wave of relief as she ascertained her brother's safety.

It'd definitely be bad if they ran into a powerful beast before even reaching the Dragon.

"So, where's the Dragon?"

"Ah, hold on. It's uhh… Here. Yeah, the rocky crag to the northwest. Wait… Hold on…"

The marker on the map showed where the Dragon was, but something didn't feel right…

I squinted my eyes before pinching my fingers on the screen and zooming in.

The zoomed-in map confirmed my fears. There were two overlapping markers.

"Oh crap… There are two Dragons here!"

"What?!"

Hilde stared at my smartphone in shock. There was no mistaking it… There were two markers. It was kind of like the case with the Mithril Golem forever ago.

Even if they were Lestian knights, it'd be almost impossible for them to kill two Dragons. I wasn't sure what to do.

"…Maybe we could take one of them away from the other and let your brother fight it."

"Do you think he'd be okay?"

"Probably, yeah. It won't be an easy fight, though. It'll take them some time to ground the Dragon."

That was the most difficult part of Dragon fighting. You could use a powerful Wind spell to shred their wings, but none of the Lestian knights were specialized in that regard, as far as I knew.

Thus, they had no choice but to fight with bows and arrows, but that had challenges to it as well. If the Dragon sensed too much danger, it would just fly off. That was why it was imperative to bring it down to the ground and keep it there. Obviously, bows and arrows could bring down a Dragon with a lucky shot, but this wasn't especially reliable.

I decided we should draw one of them away, so we needed to head off immediately. We needed to do it covertly, since we didn't want to blow our cover.

The two of us made our way to the nesting grounds.

We carried on through the mountainous area, checking our smartphone maps every so often until we arrived.

The two of them were feasting on a large monster together. Both of them had Gold-Copper scales, and one of them was considerably larger than the other. *A male and a female, huh? Wonder if they're a couple…*

"They're a noble species, but it seems these ones are immature. They're talking about attacking more humans when they're done eating. Seems they find it fun. I'm glad Luli isn't here; she'd have turned the two of them into charcoal by now."

Kougyoku gave us the gist of what the two Dragons were saying. If Luli was here… That certainly would've been a problem…

I shuddered quietly, thinking about that Dragon's fire breath, when Hilde suddenly caught my attention.

"Ah, Touya... I have a request. Can you let me kill that Dragon on my own?"

"You want to do it alone?"

Hilde's face turned red. I wasn't sure why.

"This is a touch embarrassing, but... I've always wanted to kill a Dragon, as well..."

"Huh?"

"I-It's honorable for a knight to defeat a Dragon! I can't pass on this opportunity now, so please!"

"Aha... Alright, I guess."

Geez. She really is just as knightly as her brother.

I could understand her feelings well enough, so it was no big deal.

"I-I'm planning on confining one, but which one did you want to fight?"

"The big one!"

She answered without hesitation. That meant the Lestian forces would fight the smaller female...

That was probably better, actually. Hilde had been taught by the god of swords herself, so she'd be able to take on a Dragon for sure. If anything, I was more worried about the soldiers.

Better to confine the smaller one, then.

"[Prison]."

"Graaagh?!"

The Dragon was placed within a barrier, and started thrashing around. It was a waste of effort, since it wasn't gonna escape.

"Lestian Sacred Sword: First Cutter!"

"Grargh!"

Hilde slashed toward the neck of the free Dragon.

The cut was only a shallow one, but it was enough for the beast to register her as a threat.

"Graaargh!"

"Let us go!"

Hilde charged out of the rocky nesting area, causing the male Dragon to pursue her.

Once we reached an area that was easy to fight in, Hilde turned around and faced the Dragon head-on.

The Dragon suddenly opened its gaping maw. It looked like it was preparing a fire breath attack.

"GRAAARGH!"

"Mph!"

I thought the Dragon was about to spew flames, but it vomited up a streaming blast of liquid.

Hilde jumped to the side, the liquid spraying to the ground and causing it to bubble and sizzle away. I looked closer and saw that any plants in the path of the substance had been completely melted. It was some kind of potent solvent liquid, an acid spit.

That was kind of annoying. Hilde wielded a phrasium blade. It was extremely sharp and durable, but I didn't know how it'd do against acid. I'd never tested that before... I didn't think it'd melt that easily, though.

"Gra... Ragh!"

"Guh...!"

Hilde still seemed determined not to get any liquid on her sword. She continued to dodge the acid spray.

She charged forward, ducking under the acid breath and charging straight toward the Dragon.

"Lestian Sacred Sword: First Cutter!"

"Grargh!"

The wind blade from Hilde's attack sliced through one of the Dragon's wings, impairing its ability to fly. I was really impressed! I stood at the side with a double thumbs-up as the Gold-Copper Dragon fell down.

Now it's on the ground, good. It'll be easier. But even a grounded Dragon isn't so simple.

"Gragh!"

The Gold-Copper Dragon started firing out spray after spray, several blasts at once. It seemed to be able to fire multiple short blasts like a water gun.

Hilde easily dodged the attack, then charged forward again.

"Lestian Sacred Sword: Third Shear!"

Hilde jumped up and cleaved off the Dragon's wings at the base. Now it wouldn't be able to fly away at all.

"Groargh!"

The Dragon's claws swiped toward Hilde as she descended. There was nowhere for her to escape. The Dragon probably expected her to go for its wings…

"Lestian Sacred Sword: Second Wardance!"

"Gyah?!"

The sword danced, ripping the Dragon's outstretched hand to shreds. The scaly beast pulled its arm back out of pain as Hilde landed safely.

Hilde then turned backward with a flourish and cut the Dragon's tail at the tip. The Dragon furiously swung its tail, but it wasn't as fast as before. She was whittling it down.

"GRAAARGHHH!"

Looks like it's spewing acid at random... Wait, it's coming this way?!

"Touya?!"

"Ack! **[Teleport]!**" I quickly warped away from the incoming acid.

That was almost a very unlucky moment for me. A little more... and I'd have gotten burned... Though, if it hit an ordinary person, they'd have been melted into goo.

"How dare you aim for Touya!"

...I don't think it was trying to hit me specifically or anything.

Fury burned in Hilde's eyes as she faced down the Dragon. It kept on spitting more globs of acid to prevent her advance, but she kept on dodging, left to right.

Hilde jumped right up in front of the Dragon, scorn burning through her very being.

"Lestian Sacred Sword: Fifth Swirl!"

Hilde's spinning blade aimed right for the Dragon's chest.

"Gragh... Frugh...!"

"It's over."

Hilde's crystal blade flashed in the air, slashing upward and digging into the Dragon's throat. The Dragon's head fell to the ground, its long neck swaying left and right as it oozed blood.

Done already? She killed it pretty fast.

Hilde sheathed her blade as I walked over to her.

"Good work, Hilde. You killed it!"

"Yes! I'm really pleased!"

Kind of a shame this wasn't a guild mission, though. With just me as a witness, she might not get the Dragonslayer title.

Then again, I'm a Gold adventurer, so my testimony should be enough. I'll ask Relisha to be on the safe side. Plus, the dead Dragon should be proof.

"Oh yeah, the other one…"

"Yeah, you're right. Let's head back."

I put the dead Dragon into [Storage] and we headed back toward the nest.

It was trapped in the barrier, still thrashing around. It seemed like it was still healthy, if not a little fatigued.

"Now, I'll just cover our tracks a little…"

I took my smartphone out and called Reinhard.

"Hey, 'sup. It's Touya. Just wanted to say that my map's telling me the Dragon's to your northwest. Also, I heard this one has acidic breath, so be careful out there! Best of luck, man."

I spoke as if I was calling from Brunhild, and he seemed convinced enough.

Now all I had to do was lead the Dragon to the Lestian knights.

"Alright, let's do this."

"Of course!"

I cast [Levitation] on Hilde, and I used [Fly] to float up alongside the [Prison]-confined Dragon.

I didn't want anyone seeing us by chance, so I cast [Mirage] to disguise us as eagles against the night sky.

Now all I had to do was release the barrier.

"Graaarrrggghhh!"

"Shut up."

"Groagh?!"

The Dragon roared before being smacked across the face by Hilde. From the perspective of an onlooker, it would've looked like an eagle swiping its talons at the monster.

"Let's go, then!"

"GRARGHGRAAAAAAGH!"

We flew off, and the Gold-Copper Dragon immediately gave chase. But we just kept on flying slowly but surely toward the Lestian knights.

The moment we saw the group of knights in the forest below, I cast **[Invisible]** on Hilde and myself.

The knights were focused on the Dragon, so it didn't pay any heed to the mysterious vanishing eagles up above.

"Archers, take aim!"

Arrows rained from below, and I decided to give them a helping hand. I snapped one of the Dragon's wing tendons with Wind magic.

"Gragh?!"

It was unable to maintain its balance, so it tumbled downward.

That was the full extent of my interference, though. I wanted to see how Reinhard and the Lestian knights fared against the Dragon.

"Lestian Sacred Sword: Sixth Roaring Thunder!"

"Graaah!"

Reinhard's crystal blade stabbed through the Dragon's brain.

The Gold-Copper Dragon seized up, and its head fell to the ground with a mighty crash.

"We… did it? We did it! The Dragon's dead!"

Reinhard raised his sword after pulling it out of the Dragon's head. The small group of Lestian knights alongside him cheered at the sight. Some cried with joy, some fell to their knees with exhaustion, and some jumped around happily.

Lestian tradition said it was honorable for a knight to slay a Dragon. But the chances to do so were sparse, and when they came up, they were extremely deadly.

I wondered how they felt after such an ordeal. They were lucky that they'd all survived. There were a good few injured, but none were dead.

Reinhard took a selfie next to the dead Dragon's head. He seemed to be treating all this pretty casually, but I could tell he was happy.

Hilde and I received a text with the photo attachment shortly afterward. Reinhard was smiling wide in the picture, so he must've been totally overjoyed. I immediately texted him back to congratulate him.

"Kinda funny getting a text from him when he's right there, huh? What do you think…? Wait, Hilde?!"

I turned around and saw Hilde openly weeping at her phone. She looked up, showing her streaming tears and runny nose.

"Sniff… My brother… Ahhh, my brother… He… Ah… He's so happy… Thank you!"

I wanted to give her a big hug, but the crying was a little extreme. If we stayed in the vicinity, I was sure they'd hear us.

"[Gate]!"

I opened up a portal and warped right in front of Reinhard. I figured it'd be better to pretend we'd warped right over from Brunhild to congratulate him.

"Hilde?!"

"Brother!"

Hilde nestled her face into Reinhard's chest.

"Congratulations… You fought so hard!"

"…Thank you, Hilde."

Reinhard gently pet Hilde on the head.

The girl I looked at wasn't a knight princess, just a sister truly happy for her brother. Hilde knew exactly how much this meant to Reinhard, so she was legitimately proud that he'd made a childhood dream come true.

"You'll get Dragon's blood on you. You should move back a little."

"You're right…"

Hilde finally parted from her brother. I handed over a handkerchief to her and she wiped her face.

Reinhard smiled over toward his sister, then turned to me.

"Grand Duke, if you could…"

"You want me to carry the Dragon back? No problem, I'm on it. I'll send you all back to Lestia's capital while I'm at it."

"Thank you."

I shoved the dead Dragon into [Storage] and opened up a [Gate] back to the castle courtyard in Lestia. When we were back, I took out the Dragon from [Storage], taking care not to bring out the wrong one. And when I brought it out, everyone nearby started to cheer.

Hilde and Reinhard's parents came out into the courtyard along with their grandpa, Galen.

"Ohoho… You really did it, Reinhard."

"I did, grandfather."

The old man grinned broadly as he struck his cane against the Dragon's corpse.

"A Gold-Copper, eh? That's quite the apex predator. Did the Grand Duke help, I wonder?"

"No, I just carried it back. The Lestian forces are the ones that killed it."

"Is that right? Incredible work, son."

The former king patted his son on the shoulder. He laughed heartily, causing Reinhard to breathe a sigh of relief.

"Now now, it wasn't just me. I won thanks to the support of my men."

"Mmm. Keep that spirit with you. You've truly grown as a knight today."

"Indeed!"

Hrmph… It's a touching scene, but nobody here knows his sister killed an even bigger one earlier. Obviously, I'm not gonna say anything, though.

After the initial fuss was made, the story of Reinhard and his brave men was made public. The entire city quickly started singing its praises of the knight king, and the streets were packed with celebrating commoners. I was pretty surprised by the commotion, given that I was so overpowered at this point that I'd just hunt Dragons for their meat or whatever.

Well, at any rate, Reinhard could call himself a true Dragonslayer now. I helped a little by grounding the Dragon, but the kill was all on the rest of them.

"The king and his men have slain a foul beast!"

"Hail the Dragonslayer!"

"All hail the king!"

Hilde and her brother stood by the gates as the townsfolk cheered.

"Wanna get your Dragonslayer title from the guild?" I whispered.

The dead Dragon was still in my [Storage]. With that and my own testimony, I was sure she'd get the title. In retrospect, I should've just recorded a video.

"…No need. I'm happy just having that memory with you, Touya. I'm glad we got to see my brother kill a Dragon and that he could do so safely and brilliantly."

"Oh, I see…"

That was just like her. Hilde was that kind of person, through and through. She didn't care about the title at all; she just wanted to make sure the second Dragon wouldn't give her brother a hard time. She'd done it again, giving it her all for the sake of another. Her selfless nature was one of the things I loved the most about her.

"We should make something from the Dragon you killed to commemorate your victory, anyway. Maybe some armor or a shield?"

"Actually, I want to stuff and mount its head as a bedroom decoration."

"Really?"

...*Mounting it like a hunting trophy? Well, I guess that's alright.*

"Sure... But will there be room?"

"It should be fine. I don't have much in my room."

Each of my fiancees had their own bedroom, and they were fairly large ones. Each was decorated differently, and all had their own charm.

Linze's room had stuffed toys and sewing gear all around, while Yae's room had tatami mats and had a more Eashenese aesthetic.

Hilde's room had swords and armor pieces in the corners, but she was pretty space-efficient in general. It was likely that there'd be room on the walls for a hunting trophy. It would probably be fine.

Personally, if I woke up in the middle of the night and saw a Dragon's head on the wall, I'd probably be inclined to freak out.

"Well, that should be okay..."

"Thank you."

I was a little confused by her aesthetic taste, but it was her call at the end of the day.

"Oooh! Th-That's amazing! It's like it's really alive!"

Sue gazed up in awe at the mounted Dragon's head on the wall. Honestly, it kind of felt like an actual Dragon was peeking its head into the room…

Doctor Babylon helped us stuff the head, but it still felt a little out of place.

"A… Ahaha… It certainly has a presence, huh…?"

"Y-Yes, it's quite something…"

Yumina and Linze looked up at it uneasily. The two of them seemed to share my feelings on it, but quite a few of the girls were excited.

"Ooh! It is truly impressive, it is! I wish I had one too, I do!"

"Yeah, I'm a little jealous… But a Dragon head wouldn't suit my room, I think."

Yae and Elze looked up at the head with impressed smiles on their faces. I had a feeling that the two of them would be in full support of Hilde's new decoration.

Elze's room had a lot of surprisingly cute stuff in it, so a stuffed Dragon head wouldn't support the aesthetic. It definitely wouldn't suit the Eashen feeling of Yae's room, either.

"Touya-dono! I wish to hunt a Dragon as well, I do!"

"Yeah, I want in as well!"

Yae and Elze both turned toward me. I didn't really see a point... They already had the Dragonslayer title, anyway.

"I really want to do this, I do! I would like to hunt a suitable trophy, I would!"

"Yeah! We could decorate the castle entryway!"

I wasn't really sure about that plan, since we'd probably scare any guests who came by.

"...There's like a whole graveyard's worth of dead Dragons in my **[Storage]**, you know...? We can just use those if you care so much..."

"No way! That's no good at all!"

"Indeed! I want it to be the fruit of my own hunt, I do!"

I was trapped.

Aaagh, at this rate, I'm gonna have to go out Dragon hunting again... Why did it come to this?

Despite my exasperated sigh, Hilde walked over to me and simply smiled.

The discussion between Refreese and Panaches went without issue. They established a clear border between their territories and established friendly trade.

The people of the regular world didn't know what Gollems were, and the people of the Reverse World were mostly unfamiliar with magic. And so, in order to reconcile these differences, the world leaders needed to take the initiative. Panaches decided to send some work Gollems and engineers to Refreese, and Refreese would send some magic scholars and books over in return. I hoped that the cultural exchange would enrich both nations.

I'd received an information report from Anubis and Bastet, who were both still in Isengard. Since the divine venom didn't affect regular humans, and they couldn't even see it, life was actually continuing pretty ordinarily over there.

At the time of their report, the two Gollems were in a port town to the east of the country. They'd heard rumors that some of the more inland towns had been destroyed by golden monsters, and that the knight order and Gollem squad had been sent out to deal with them. Bastet and Anubis were set to leave the town shortly after their report, their next destination a larger settlement near the heart of the island.

After I received that report, I headed off to consult Elluka about what I'd heard from Blau about the white crown.

"We met Noir quite by coincidence. The crown Gollems were all unearthed in ancient research facilities, or ruins of particular note… But not Noir. We found that one in a mine."

"Really?"

"Yep. A leylightstone mine. It was one that had been abandoned for quite some time. I originally thought we'd found some decommissioned mining Gollem, but when I saw the crown series emblem on its neck, I knew exactly what we'd stumbled upon."

Elluka apparently set to work repairing Noir immediately, but it took her a considerable amount of time. After a year, the repairs were complete, but Noir refused to contract with her.

"Crowns are picky when it comes to their masters. I just didn't have the right qualities, you know? Then, when I went out on a trip, my sister snuck into the lab and, well… the rest is history."

Elluka shrugged a bit as she sipped her coffee. I wondered if the crown Gollems had special qualities they looked for when it came to their masters. The black crown had Norn, the red had Nia, the blue had Robert, and the purple chose Luna…

I couldn't really think of anything connecting them… besides the fact that most of them were pretty annoying at times.

From what I understood, the blue crown was passed down the Panaches family line, and the former master of the red crown was Nia's dad. It might have been a genetic thing.

"Actually, the circumstances in which we found Noir were a little odd."

"How do you mean?"

"Well, typically, you unearth legacy Gollems inside the earth, or deep inside ancient scientific facilities. But with Noir, it was carelessly discarded in a mineshaft, one that wasn't even ancient!

If you consider that it was a closed-down mineshaft, then it must have had workers in it, right?"

"Which means Noir must have been put there after the mine closed... Or Noir walked there and shut down."

"It's also possible that someone forced it into shutdown mode."

According to Blau, Noir should've been with the white crown. I wondered if Albus, the white crown, had been the one to force its other half into shutdown... It didn't show up anywhere when I used my search magic, even though it should've just resembled a white version of Noir or Rouge. There shouldn't have been anything stopping me from finding it.

Basically, there was either something blocking my spell... or the white crown was just gone entirely...

Either way, worrying wasn't going to solve anything. I decided to take it easy for a little bit.

I left Babylon and went to Brunhild's castle. After I entered the living room, I found Leen sitting there with her arms folded. Paula was sitting next to her in the same pose, but I had a feeling Leen was the only one in thought.

"Something wrong?"

"A trifling matter. I was just thinking of the magical aptitude held by the denizens of the Reverse World, compared to that of ours."

Seems like she's thinking about something complicated again... Well, I better sit down and hear her out.

"It's likely due to evolutionary differences and environmental factors. The people from the Reverse World have less magic power on average. They also have a lower amount of people with an aptitude for magic. However, their ability to manipulate magic is actually more refined, likely because they've been using magitechnology for a long time."

Oh yeah, that makes sense. Candles are still common here, but the other side has had leylightstone and stuff. You can adjust the light settings on those things by tweaking magic flow.

"So you're saying Reverse World natives aren't really good with magic?"

"Not necessarily, no. There are people from the Red Cats who wield magic well, right? The leader of the Black Cats as well, if I recall."

Well, putting Nia and her group aside, I recall helping with Silhouette's summoning ritual…

"I'm sure the difference will become less important as time goes on and both sides mingle and reproduce. The people of our grandchildren's grandchildren's grandchildren's generation will likely be on common ground."

"That's quite a while away."

"Oh, are you sure? You're a god-to-be, and I'm part of a long-lived species. Such a period may well be a blink of an eye in due time."

Leen took hold of my hand. I wasn't surprised that she felt that way, given her fairy nature. She'd lived for a long time, after all.

"Our grandchildren's grandchildren's grandchildren, huh…? That's pretty hard to imagine."

"Our children will have fairy blood, so they'll live quite a long time as well."

The children of a fairy and a human didn't take on characteristics of both parents like half-elves; they'd always come out full fairy. The same could be said of Sakura, as well. Any kids I had with her would come out demonkin of the overlord's lineage.

The fairy race also had an extremely low male birth rate. There was only around a twenty percent chance that fairy children would be boys.

God also informed me that my kids would effectively be demi-gods. They'd have longer-than-average lifespans compared to regular humans, but that'd only bring them to maybe living twice as long as their peers. Their kids would have lesser lifespans as the divine blood ended up being diluted. My grandchildren and great-grandchildren would probably have standard human lifespans.

Either way, my children with Leen and Sakura would live the longest.

"Seems we'll be together a long time, eh?"

"I'm a little worried, though... If my daughter physically develops before her body stops changing... she might end up looking older than me for the rest of our lives!" Leen grumbled quietly. That was certainly possible. Leen's body made her look like a twelve-year-old. Physically, she didn't look that much older than Sue. But since her body wouldn't grow more, that meant Sue would eventually overtake her.

According to God Almighty, the divinity granted to my fiancees would halt their aging once they reached a certain point in adulthood, but Leen was already an adult by the standards of her race. She was probably a little insecure about her looks and hadn't quite come to terms with the fact that she didn't have the body she wanted.

"C'mon, don't worry about things like that. I love you for who you are, Leen. So I'll be by your side no matter what."

"That's not really the issue... Agh... Well, no matter. It's pointless to envy a daughter that hasn't yet been born."

Leen chuckled softly before reaching up to give me a hug and a kiss. I wrapped my arms around her delicate body in turn, giving her a quick squeeze.

"I'll be fine enough if you keep on giving me all your love... I don't want to get jealous if you fawn over our daughter, after all..."

"I-I'll try my best... Ahaha, that probably sounded lame..."

"My, you really are a troublesome man... I don't mind, though."

I was glad she was so calm around me. I didn't really think she needed to get jealous of our kid. The love between a man and his wife was different from the love between a father and his daughter, anyway. That reminded me, though...

"Leen, this might be a bit late to ask, but... do you have any siblings? And are your parents still around?"

"It definitely is a bit late to ask."

Leen grinned, teasing a wink my way. I kind of always had the image of Leen's parents being dead already, since she was the matriarch of the fairies.

"I have no siblings. Races with such long lifespans have a low conception rate, and by nature, we're a curious species. For the majority of our lives, we go around investigating things that we like. That's why, when it comes down to actually trying for a baby, it's usually just the one."

I wondered if that wouldn't eventually lead to their extinction, but it seemed like their long lifespans kept that balanced, somehow...

"And your parents?"

"My parents are in Avalon right now. It's a realm where many fairies dwell after reaching a certain age."

Avalon was a separate pocket of reality you could get to from the Sea of Trees. It was functionally similar to the spirit realm, apparently. Older fairies often made the pilgrimage to Avalon and lived their last few hundred years there in peace.

"My parents will likely never return from Avalon, but I think they're probably still alive."

"Isn't that a bit…?"

"It's nothing to worry about. I said my tearful goodbyes to my parents a few hundred years ago, and I have a new family now."

Leen smiled sincerely. I couldn't detect any sadness at all. The Avalon stuff was probably just regular business to the fairies.

"…I kinda wanted to meet your parents, to be honest."

"Well, I'd have certainly liked to meet your parents as well…"

Given that I have godlike powers, it wouldn't be impossible to return back to Earth. But I'm technically definitely dead there… If I want to introduce Leen to my parents, the best I can probably do is stand by their beds like a ghost or something. But if they woke up and saw that, they'd die from shock themselves. Maybe I can visit them in a dream sequence or something… Man, this is kind of a weird topic.

Well whatever, no point worrying about the impossible! As if to break the solemn silence, my phone began to vibrate. I had an incoming call from commander Lain. I wondered what was up.

"'Sup?"

"This is Lain. There's someone at the gates calling himself a friend of yours…"

"A friend, huh?"

I wondered who it was. If it was Zanac or Micah, then Lain should've been familiar with them… Maybe it was Ende?

"Well, he's… How can I put this without seeming rude…? He's wearing… interesting clothing. He also has a tiny crown on his head, and he's calling himself a prince?"

"Oh, I know who it is. I'll be down in a sec."

Well, there's nobody else it could be with a description like that. Guess His Royal Doofus teleported over. At least give me some warning before you… Oh! I checked my texts and saw that he'd actually sent me a message.

It seemed like he'd actually taken my advice to heart about only texting me if it was important. Though he hadn't exactly given me too much warning. The text came three minutes before he arrived…

"Is it the prince you brought up earlier?" Leen crooked a brow.

"Yeah. It's my first time being on the other side of a guy just appearing out of nowhere with a teleportation power, so I guess I was reflecting on the inconveniences I might've caused in the past."

…*Well, in my case, I always try to notify people beforehand. Mostly. For the most part… When I can, I mean… Most of the time, it's during emergencies!*

"Wanna come with me, Leen? I can introduce you to him."

"Sure thing. I'm a little curious about him. Come along, Paula."

Paula rolled over and grabbed on to my ankle.

I held Leen close and invoked [**Teleport**]**,** taking us to Lain.

As I'd expected, the boy in front of us was the prince. A short cape, bob-cut blond hair, white tights, and pumpkin pants. It was Robert.

"Hey, Touya! We're here!"

"Not sounding so princely right now, are you…?"

I would've given him a soft chop on the forehead, but he'd brought guests. Obviously one of them was his Gollem, Blau. They wouldn't have been able to come without invoking its power, after all.

The other guest was a girl in a pretty dress. Her hair was long and lovely, and her adoring gaze was well and truly fixed on the prince.

The girl was Robert's fiancee, Cerestia Twente Hernandez. I'd met her a few days ago and handed over a smartphone to her. She was the Queen of Strain's niece, making her genuine royalty.

Ceres accepted all of Robert, despite his weird attitude and fashion sense. She was really the best partner possible for him.

It was a little rude of me, but I had some initial doubts about how legitimate her love for him was... Though it seemed like she really loved him. Different strokes for different folks, as they say.

"Ah, Touya. Thank you so much for that gift the other day. I can speak with Robert on a daily basis now. It's so wonderful!"

"I'm just glad you like it."

Ceres smiled widely as she flashed the mass-produced smartphone my way.

The two of them were escorted by four guards, but there was another young man with them as well. He didn't seem that far from me or Robert in terms of age. His eyes were golden, and his hair was ashen-grey. His ears were pointed, and his tanned skin had splotches of scales covering it. Two horns sprouted from his scalp, and he had a lizard-like tail.

"Are you... dragonkin?" Leen spoke up. She was the court magician of Mismede once, so it stood to reason that she'd be curious about his race.

"Dragonkin? I don't know of that race... I'm a dragonewt. We dragonewt have inherited draconic power. It marks our lineage as the Grand Potentate's flesh and blood."

Dragonewt, huh? Maybe that's what they call dragonkin in the Reverse World... He looks pretty similar to Sonia, from my perspective.

"That's right! I brought him here to meet you, Touya! He's—"

Robert suddenly fell forward and landed on his face. Then, he began snoring loudly. That was the price for using his power...

Leen and Paula stared at me with wide, confused eyes.

"Oh, don't worry about it. This is just normal for him."

Blau immediately hauled Robert over its shoulder. Ceres took out a small handkerchief and wiped the sleeping beauty's face clean of dirt. How very dutiful of them...

"Forgive us, please. Could we have a room with a bed? He should wake up in around four hours."

He sure likes his naps... I didn't mind letting them have a room, so I told Lain to show them to a vacant one.

Blau left with Robert, his guards in tow. Ceres cleared her throat and gestured toward the dragonkin... Er, I mean, dragonewt.

"I'll introduce him in Robert's stead. This is Zanbelt Gal Lassei. He's the second prince of the Lassei Military Kingdom."

Zanbelt bowed his head softly.

...Oh. The prince brought me another prince.

The Lassei Military Kingdom.

It was a nation north of Isengard and west of Strain. The country was multicultural and valued a powerful military over all else.

If I had to pick an equivalent country, it'd probably be Mismede. There were all kinds of races living harmoniously in that country, but the most interesting thing about them was their national culture.

They were referred to as the Military Kingdom, which clearly meant its people prized strength over all else. But it wasn't just physical strength. They also strove for mental strength.

In short, they respected people who honed both body and mind.

It was fine to have a strong body, but to have a truly strong mind, one would also need to empathize with others. They were the living personification of the phrase, "a healthy mind in a healthy body."

Putting Gollems aside, they were the strongest country in the world.

A quote from a famous piece of detective fiction came to mind...
"If I wasn't hard, I wouldn't be alive. If I couldn't ever be gentle,
I wouldn't deserve to be alive."

As for the reason the second Prince of Lassei decided to visit us?

"I wish to face the strongest person in this nation. My father has
granted me permission."

"Wait, wait... Hold up. No holding back? Dude, you'll die."

*The strongest in this country... That's probably Moroha or
Takeru. Going up against either one of them is basically suicide, and
I'd rather not have foreign blood on my hands.*

The second prince of Lassei, Zanbelt Gal Lassei, seemingly took
offense to what I had said.

"I am the second prince of a proud military kingdom. I am
certain that my strength puts me in the top five of my entire nation,
so I do not believe I would lose so easily to any foe. If you wish to
decline my offer because you fear a loss, I'd appreciate you being
honest."

*That's definitely not why I'm declining, man... Ugh, what do
I do?*

"If he says he wants to fight, why not allow it? Since he brought
up the challenge, he won't be able to complain when he loses, right?"

Zanbelt's brow twitched a bit in response to Leen's words.
I wondered if she was trying to egg him on intentionally...

"What's your fighting style, Prince Zanbelt?"

"I am adept in all forms of combat, but my preference is hand-
to-hand brawling."

*I see... That'd probably mean Takeru's his best bet. Given that
he's the god of combat, that would make them an interesting match.*

"And you're sure about this? You don't plan on backing down?"

"Not in the least! I wish to fight against the strongest around in order to hone my skills! That's a warrior's greatest joy!"

Prince Zanbelt grinned broadly as he spoke. I was worried he wouldn't have the chance to throw a single punch…

"Wahaha! What a hot-blooded young'un! I'll be glad to pummel you!"

Uncle Takeru grinned, sending wild laughter echoing around the northern training grounds. Ende and Elze stood by my side, displaying the same forced smile I had. Moroha stood by grinning even more madly than Takeru. She'd volunteered to be the referee. Leen sat on a nearby bench, casually reading a book. Paula seemed pretty hyped up, though.

Robert's fiancee, Ceres, wasn't interested in the fight at all. She'd walked off to Robert's bedroom instead.

Apparently, she loved to spend her time watching Robert's face as he slept. She certainly had unusual taste… But given Robert's own unusual taste, that probably made them a good match.

"How long do you think he'll last?"

"That depends on Master, I think."

"Yeah, you're right. I don't think he'll go all-out on the prince…"

Ende, Elze, and I were both chatting amongst ourselves about the fight. The prince narrowed his eyes and glanced my way. It seemed like he had a keen sense of hearing.

"I, Prince Zanbelt Gal Lassei, will fight with the military arts my nation taught me! Let us begin!"

"Good hustle, kiddo! Then I, Mochizuki Takeru, will face you!"

"Ready? Fight!"

At Moroha's command, the battle began. In less than the blink of an eye, we heard a thwacking sound, and Prince Zanbelt went flying backward at incredible speeds. He rolled on the ground and started twitching. Takeru had hit him in the chest with an elbow strike.

Elze, Ende, and I cried out in utter disbelief. *What the hell was that?!*

We ran up to Prince Zanbelt in a panic. He had foam coming out of his mouth, and his eyes had rolled back into his head.

"Were you trying to kill him or something?!"

"Wahahaha! No way! If I wanted him dead I'd have plucked his heart out of his body! I held back just enough that he's simply on the verge of death! His heart might've stopped a little bit, but some Restoration magic will fix him right up!"

Wait, no! If he needs Healing magic to survive, then you already did too much! I freaked out and cast **[Cure Heal]** on Zanbelt. The prince promptly opened his eyes.

"Augh! Waugh! Wh-What was?! What happened?!"

"My uncle took you out in one shot... Don't you remember?"

"N-No! Th-That's impossible, I couldn't have been beaten so easily!"

The prince fell to his knees in disbelief.

"That was a little dull, Takeru. You should've played with him a bit longer."

"If his block game was that bad the entire match, he wouldn't have lasted long! I certainly don't think he'd have lived up to your hopes, Moroha!"

"W-Wait! Please let me try again!"

Zanbelt butted in on the exchange between the two gods.

"Hm. Again, huh? Got a plan? Otherwise, it'll just be a repeat of what just happened."

"Yes! I'll unleash the true power of the dragonewt! I cannot possibly lose!"

"Hoh… The dragonewt's power, eh? Color me intrigued… I'll fight you once more, then!"

Both parties agreed, so we decided to start again from the top. I wished the guy would just give up, though…

"HAAAAAAAAAAAAAAAHHH!"

"Oh?"

Zanbelt took a combative stance, and a chi-like energy began swaying around his body. His muscles beefed up, and scales spread out all across his skin.

"Oh, is that fighting spirit?"

"Yup, it's fighting spirit."

Ende and Elze looked quite surprised. Apparently, fighting spirit was a method of dispersing magical energy throughout your own body and using it to change your physical characteristics. Sonia's ability to release stored power was a similar application of this ability. Given that she was of the dragon clan, and Zanbelt was of the dragonewt, it wasn't too surprising they had similar abilities.

"Attacks like your earlier one won't work anymore! I have assumed the form of a valiant Dracul! My speed, strength, and durability are far higher than they once were!"

Zanbelt punctuated his sentence with a beastly roar.

"Ready? Fight!"

At Moroha's command, the battle began. In less than the blink of an eye, we heard a thwacking sound, and Prince Zanbelt went flying backward at incredible speeds. He rolled on the ground and started twitching.

"IT HAPPENED AGAIN?!"

Nothing changed?! That part was basically identical! We rushed over to Prince Zanbelt in a panic. He had foam coming out of his mouth, and his eyes had rolled back into his head. Again. I cast **[Cure Heal]**.

"What?! Huh? I, what...?"

"My uncle took you out in one shot... Again."

"N-No! Th-That's impossible. I was a Dracul this time! I couldn't have been beaten so easily!"

The prince fell to his knees in disbelief. Again.

"Guh... I accept my loss!"

"...Yeah."

I didn't really know what to say to him. Saying something like, "You did well," or "You tried" wouldn't work, since he didn't get to do a thing.

I decided to turn to Takeru for commentary. He was an adult, so he'd probably be able to say something more inspiring.

"So... how was he as a foe?"

"Completely worthless!"

You're crushing him here! Throw him a bone! I-I get why you said it, but still... You didn't really give him a chance to do anything.

Zanbelt raised his head slightly, then crawled toward Takeru before bowing his head.

"I-I admit my loss! But that power you wield... It's as if you're a combat god! It's far beyond my level... So far beyond... I beg of you, please take me as your disciple!"

"Heck no!"

Please stop trampling on his heart! At least pretend like you thought about it! He looks seriously upset!

"Isn't it possible to take him on? You took Ende and Elze, didn't you?"

"Ende is a person I scouted myself, and Elze benefits from certain qualities you bear. Compared to those two, this little squirt isn't worth writing home about. Can't exactly teach a little baby about arithmetic, right?"

"A-Are you saying I'm weaker than those two?!"

Prince Zanbelt desperately pointed at Ende and Elze. It was probably hard for him to accept that those two were Takeru's disciples.

"You couldn't even judge my strength properly. If you can't appraise based on posture and appearance, you'll get embarrassingly defeated someday!"

Someday? That just happened, didn't it?

Prince Zanbelt glared over at Ende and Elze with fire in his eyes.

Hey, easy now… It's not their fault he turned you down.

"Th-Then how about this?! If I can defeat either one of those two, will you take me on as your disciple?"

"Sure."

"Perfect! It's a deal!"

The two of them let out small exasperated whines when they heard Takeru's swift declaration. I could understand their feelings.

"Ende, Elze. If you go easy on him, tomorrow's training is gonna be a full course of extra-hard work."

The two of them shrieked softly and went pale in the face. I was a little worried about what kind of training he'd been putting them through…

"Whichever of you beats him the fastest gets a break tomorrow afternoon."

"Hell yeah!"

The two of them cheered in unison. I really, REALLY worried about their training regimen.

After that, he fought them one after the other… and he lost just about as quickly as he lost against Takeru. I didn't really have any comments left to give at this point. Using my Restoration magic on the prince was starting to feel like a chore.

The one who got the afternoon break ended up being Ende. That bastard should've let Elze win! I felt kind of bad for her.

In the end, Zanbelt demanded a fight with me, but I was so tired of the process by then that I just punched him and sent him flying off into the sky. It took a while to sink in, but I started to realize that Prince Zanbelt was actually kind of an idiot.

"This can't be… I'm a proud dragonewt… Dragon blood flows within me… How could I lose to mere humans? The humans in this country… are far too unusual!"

Zanbelt was on the ground, staring at the floor and muttering. *Nothing mere about the humans here, Prince.*

"Listen, kiddo. You gotta discard the crap about being a proud dragonewt and things about it being impossible to lose to humans. Pride is one thing, arrogance is another. Thoughts like that won't make you any stronger."

The prince raised his head when Takeru started speaking. He'd been beaten so thoroughly that his clothes were tattered and torn. My Restoration magic only healed his body, not his possessions.

"If you keep talking about your own strength without considering the might of your enemies, then it screams inner weakness and insecurity. That's exactly how you looked to me. Easy to break. Weak."

"Guh…"

"But if you're faced with that weakness and you decide to tackle it, then you can become a strong man. You've been given that chance with this defeat, understand? You now have the choice to make use of it, or put it to waste."

"M-Master…"

I didn't know why the prince was so overcome with emotion… I thought he was putting a little too much philosophical stock in Takeru's words.

The gods didn't usually handle things all that well, to be honest. It was more likely that Takeru just said all that stuff since it felt like something smart, rather than actually saying it because he was smart.

"Oh right, what'd you even come here for? It wasn't just to fight, was it?"

"O-Oh, right. M-My father entrusted me with this letter. Here…"

Thanks to Elze's question, Zanbelt suddenly remembered his original purpose in coming to Brunhild. He took out a crumpled up letter from his pocket… that he really should've given me to begin with.

I opened the letter and it contained a notice that the Grand Potentate of Lassei would be participating in the upcoming world conference at Brunhild. He also asked us if we'd be able to chip away at the pride of his arrogant son a bit.

I think we managed more than chipping away… The boy's arrogance had basically imploded. Still, since the king asked us to do that in the first place, it'd probably be fine. They were quite the spartan family, though. Their family motto was probably something like, "Strength above all else!"

"I have a better grasp of my own weaknesses. I shall etch those words of yours into my heart, Master. I will continue to train hard starting tomorrow. Thank you so much for your guidance!"

"Mmph. I ain't making you my disciple, kiddo. But I invite you to come back once you think you're stronger. I promise to break your spirit even harder next time."

...Are you sure you're not a demon instead of a god? This is kind of like a lion cub getting pushed down a mountain, enduring hardship to make it all the way back up, then the parent pushing the cub back down again...

I felt like Takeru would toss boulders down the mountain for extra effect. Either way, it seemed like Lassei would be joining us for the summit. It was going to be more like a party than a formal meeting, but it'd be fine.

I really hoped that the Grand Potentate wasn't as thick-skulled as his son, though...

"What good little ones you are. Here, eat up!"

"Meow!"

"Woofity woof."

The tavern owner smiled wide as she fed some leftover food to a stray cat and dog. She turned around to deal with her customers afterward.

The black cat, Bastet, and the black dog, Anubis, had successfully infiltrated Steele, the second capital of Isengard.

Taverns and inns were the best places to gather information. Their ears were on constant alert for interesting info, while they got to enjoy food left to them by kind individuals. They didn't really need to eat, though.

"...Isn't it fine if we don't eat this stuff, sis?"

"Don't turn down the kindness of strangers, dummy. Being friendly with humans will help us in our goal, anyway."

"Oh, gotcha."

Anubis chowed down on his food, shrugging internally. The food wasn't completely useless, at least, since it'd add a little extra fuel to their internal generators.

The two of them continued to pretend like they were focused on their meals as they secretly listened to their surroundings.

"Didja hear Tohnam got attacked by golden monsters?"

"Seriously? What about the knights?"

"They got roughed up something fierce, so I heard. How many towns is that now?"

"Dunno, been a lot now. Things got real bad around here since that meteor shower."

The golden monsters were likely the mutants. It seemed that many towns had been attacked recently.

"I even heard stories about golden skeletons marching around…"

"Huh, seriously? Where are they headed?"

"South, so the stories said."

"South? To Isenberg?"

Isenberg was the capital city of Isengard. Ever since that giant Gollem rampaged there, the capital had been on a downward spiral.

That wasn't the only reason for the decline, though. The death of the witch-king and his lack of a successor caused massive disorganization because the old man had been handling the government almost entirely on his own. Obviously, successor conflicts broke out, and nobles scrambled to claim all the political power they could gain. The regular people were left to their own devices.

Everyone who lost their homes, jobs, or family due to the Gollem rampage was ignored by the nobles that were meant to be helping them. In the end, there was a mass exodus from the capital. The people who left the city increased by the day, to the point where it could barely be considered a capital city anymore.

"Wonder if this is the witch-king's curse…"

"Quit it. You'll jinx us…"

"Either way, this country's basically done. We should flee to Gardio or Strain if we can… I know ships are going out right now, but I dunno how long that'll last. They'll probably abandon Isengard eventually."

The number of people fleeing Isengard increased by the day, too. The unease of the people fed into more rumors, which in turn increased unease… The whole country was screwed up.

《The skeleton story sounds worth investigating.》

《Then we're gonna go south?》

The two Gollems communicated on a quiet wavelength.

《If the rumor is true, this is the doing of those mutants. We need to head south right away, let's go.》

《Gotcha.》

Bastet and Anubis turned tail and ran out of the city. Nobody noticed them leave.

The shadow of darkness covered them, and Bastet jumped on to Anubis' back.

Anubis crouched down and sped off at insane speeds. The two creatures vanished southbound, into the black.

Unfortunately, this frequent behavior on their part led to rumors of a strangely-shaped creature speeding around the roads in the dead of night. The population of Isengard was further demoralized by the thought.

"I can't say I understand, but it seems all's well that ends well!"

Robert had finally woken up from his slumber. It had been two hours since Prince Zanbelt challenged and lost to Yae, Hilde, and Lu. Losing to so many one after the other would naturally make one think that the Lassei Military Kingdom was lacking in strength, but the real reason was that my fiancees were too beyond the human norm... They were at the point where they could kill elder dragons alone with little issue.

I felt a little bad for thinking so, but I firmly believed half of the knights in our order could probably trounce Zanbelt as well. They'd been rigorously training under Moroha, after all.

I expected Prince Zanbelt, who basically had his dreams shredded and stomped on and burned, to get depressed. However, he somehow bounced back the other way completely and got really pumped up. By the last fight, it almost seemed like he expected to lose, but he went into it happily. And then, by the end...

"Now I understand just how weak my body truly is! I know now that I must train even harder!"

He spoke merrily, a strangely optimistic expression on his face. I neglected to comment, since he seemed happy enough. And after that, I passed him a response letter to the Grand Potentate of Lassei, and the group returned home thanks to Blau's power.

Robert'll be due another nap when he gets home. That power really is a blessing and a curse.

We turned to head back to the castle when my phone suddenly started vibrating. I had a call from the King of Egret, Lefang. I wondered what was up; maybe another Tentacular issue?

"Hey, 'sup. Need something?"

"Ah, Grand Duke! Sorry for the bother, but could you swing by?"

"What's going on?"

"There's an unidentified vessel approaching my nation from the southwest. Our Luphu scouts reported from above, and it seems to be an armed ship."

The Luphu were giant birds used by Egret. I wondered if the vessel was a pirate ship or some kind of warship...

Southwest, huh...? On the new map, the only country in that direction from Egret is Helgaia, Land of Fiends.

When I first learned the two worlds would merge, I researched the Reverse World nations I hadn't been to. Silhouette and her Black Cats were instrumental in me learning even more, which was why I knew a good deal about Helgaia.

It was a country populated by demi-humans referred to as fiends.

These 'fiends' were just what the Reverse World called demonkin. Stuff like werewolves, alraune, vampires, and ogres. They were humanoids with more monstrous qualities than regular beast-people. Unlike goblins, kobolds, and minotaurs, these were fairly intelligent people that established their own culture. But, much like the demonkin of my home, the fiends were persecuted throughout history for their inherent qualities.

Eventually, a vampire proclaimed himself the archfiend and founded Helgaia, a safe haven for the fiends. Several nations found the idea of a fiend nation disturbing and declared war. But the archfiend fought all of them back until they gave up.

The number of fiends (demonkin) in the Reverse World was pretty small as a result. Basically all of them lived in Helgaia. That was consistent with my experience, since I hadn't seen a single demonkin-like person at all over there.

Helgaia was smaller than Xenoahs, and it had a climate much like Egret's. It was a tropical paradise that allowed the fiends to live there peacefully, apparently.

I wondered if this incoming warship was actually from Helgaia... I was under the impression that Helgaia was much like Xenoahs when it came to conflict and outside communication. That they'd retaliate against offensive acts, but wouldn't start fights themselves...

Either way, I couldn't just leave the situation unaddressed.

"Sorry for the hassle. I just figured since the enemy's coming from the other side, it'd be better to have you here. You're the mediator, after all."

"I don't remember signing up to be the mediator..."

I sat on the beautiful shores of Egret and used a divine-infused [**Long Sense**] to check out the incoming vessel.

There was definitely a ship headed our way. Two of them, actually. They were jet black and lined with cannons. Kind of reminded me of the black ships approaching Japan under Commodore Perry... The ship had a sail, but there were also two large wheels on either side. There weren't any chimneys, but it really did resemble a steamboat. There wasn't any steam, though.

It was probably a ship that used Gollem technology.

I could see an emblem of sorts painted on the sail, which was perhaps the national emblem of Helgaia.

"I can't say for sure if they're here to attack or not. What do we do?"

"Hmm... My people are concerned, either way. We need to determine what it is they want."

The King of Egret folded his arms and pondered. He really was a large man, with well-toned muscles and tattoos all over his body. Today, he was wearing a garb that kind of reminded me of stereotypical Native American wear. He glared out to the sea in thought.

"Why don't we send them a request to stop their advance? If they don't listen, it should prove they have no intention of negotiating."

Hilde, who had been quiet up until now, raised a good point. We could determine our course of action based on how they responded to that simple request.

"And if they attack?" asked Elze, who was also accompanying me on the mission.

"Well, I don't think Egret would want us to sit back and take a beating, right? Though we should aim to capture them instead of killing them. Don't want to burn diplomatic bridges entirely."

"Mm. I agree with the Grand Duke. But if we determine that they've come here to declare war, then we needn't hold back against them."

The king and I seemed to agree, for the most part.

Helgaia didn't seem like the kind of country to randomly declare war, so I was sure it wouldn't need to come to bloodshed.

"I'll go over and try to talk to them."

I cast [Fly] and shot off from the beach. When I made it to the airspace above both ships, I used [Speaker] and cleared my throat, broadcasting my voice to the surrounding area.

"Attention, attention. Black ships, do you hear me? You are steadily approaching waters belonging to the Kingdom of Egret. Please stop your ships at once, and we will send out a messenger to—Augh!"

One of the cannons suddenly fired at me mid-sentence... *Well, that's certainly unfriendly. I get that I made a suspicious entrance, but isn't that a bit of an overreaction?*

"I'll ignore the fact that you just fired on me, but any further attacks will be regarded as a declaration of hostility. First off, we want to know your intentions in these waters. Allow me to repeat myself. Please stop your ships, and listen to us. We'd like to open up talks w—"

As I continued talking, a guy on one of the decks below pointed up and me and shouted orders to his men. Right after that, two more cannonballs came flying my way.

Goddammit, they really aren't interested in talking, huh? Are they that desperate to fight? I could hear a few people on the ship decks yelling to prepare more cannons and knock me down.

Well, if it's capture you want... I'll make you suffer a bit first.

"Come forth, Dark! I seek an Abyssal Conqueror: [Kraken]!"

Two massive shadows appeared beneath the ships. Writhing tentacles rose from the depths, lifting both ships into the air. The people on deck started running around in a panic.

The Krakens latched themselves to the backs of the ships, impeding their movement. I telepathically communicated with them and explicitly instructed them not to damage or destroy the ships. But I wasn't quite done messing with them.

"Come forth, Dark! I seek Abyssal Warriors: [Merfolk]!"

A group of fishmen rose from the deep, scaling the sides of both boats with tridents in hand. Merfolk were deep-sea monsters, but they could operate out of the water for brief periods. They were stronger in the water, but still had considerable strength outside of it.

"Eeeek!"

"Gyaaah!"

The crewmen pulled out their swords and moved to attack the Merfolk, but their blades were unable to pierce the tough scales the monsters had.

After the men were disarmed, I had the Merfolk tie them up with rope.

Once the ships were completely taken over, I noticed something interesting. Not a single member of either crew was demonkin. It seemed like these weren't Helgaian ships at all. They were just pirates.

I landed down on deck and told the Merfolk to bring me the man I'd seen barking orders earlier. He was a heavyset man with a massive beard, who resembled a stereotypical pirate in many ways...

"So you're the captain, huh? Why'd you ignore me asking you to stop?"

"J-Just who are you, huh?! One of the archfiend's trackers?!"

"The archfiend?"

Does he mean the leader of Helgaia? Are they being chased down or something? I was about to ask him for more information, but one of the Merfolk beckoned me over to the ship's hold. Non-verbal summons were kind of a pain in the ass when they needed to tell me something, but I just rolled with it. I got the gist of what they were saying, so I headed deeper into the ship.

Inside the hold, I found a cage containing three women. They were bound in iron chains. Two of them had dark skin and wore maid uniforms. They were dark elves... Probably. The third had blood-red eyes and long, silvery hair. Her skin was deathly pale, and her ears were a little pointy. I recognized her race, since my knight order had someone like her. This woman was a vampire.

She looked to be in her early twenties, but vampires lived for so long that guessing would be pointless. She was wearing a very expensive-looking dress, far higher in quality compared to the maid uniforms worn by the other two. She was probably of noble birth.

"...Who are you, exactly? I take it you're not with the pirates?"

The vampiress glared over at me with anger in her eyes. But when her gaze fell upon the Merfolk by my side, she cowered slightly. That was natural, since fish-people weren't exactly the most aesthetically appealing sight.

"My name is Mochizuki Touya. I'm the Grand Duke of Brunhild. Who are you, exactly?"

"Brunhild? I've never heard of that nation..."

"It's a little country. I wouldn't worry too much about that. Forgive me for assuming, but you seem to be a vampire. Are you from Helgaia?"

"...Indeed I am. My name is Claudia Mira Helgaia. I am the bride of Archfiend Aluford Culhat Helgaia."

Wait, what?

"So you're saying that these pirates came to Helgaia, broke out of jail... and kidnapped you?"

"Yes... I was so curious to see real live humans, so I headed down into the dungeons. Unfortunately, the pirates escaped at exactly the same time."

That was some pretty bad luck.

I'd asked Claudia, the alleged bride of Helgaia's archfiend, how she ended up with the pirates after taking her back to Egret for the time being. Even in the Reverse World, demonkin (or fiends) were discriminated against due to their frightening appearances.

From the perspective of the pirates, they'd probably entered a monster nest.

I had a feeling they escaped because they thought they'd be eaten. I guess at a glance, seeing weretigers, werewolves, and ogres would give you that impression, but all the demonkin I knew were pretty friendly people.

"So those ships were pirate vessels?"

"No, their ship was so damaged that by the time they reached Helgaia, it sank into the ocean. Those black ships were something that my husband created as part of his tinkering hobby... I didn't think they'd ever be stolen or hijacked."

His hobby?! He built those warships as part of his hobby? How much free time does he have? Oh wait, he's a vampire... He technically has all the time in the world.

The archfiend who founded Helgaia to defend the persecuted fiends was probably still the current reigning archfiend, given his vampiric nature.

Warships were probably necessary to rescue persecuted demonkin from other nations, anyway.

"So, what will happen to me now?" asked the vampiress.

"We'll make contact with your country, and arrange for you to be returned home. You're a victim in all of this, so please feel free to enjoy yourself in my kingdom until all this is dealt with."

The King of Egret spoke calmly as he sat down on his couch, causing Claudia to bow her head.

"I am humbled by your kindness, King of Egret. I was not aware that this country even existed, especially so close to Helgaia, but I truly appreciate your manners. I honestly feel a little shameful for keeping such a curious bias toward human beings..."

"Don't worry about it. Compared to demonkin... or, uh... fiends... humans are weaker on average. S'why we get around with our smarts. But that kind of ingenuity can go sour in the wrong hands, especially when coupled with prejudice or fear. It can make men like those pirates go out into the world with bad intent. I just hope you know we're not all like that."

"Of course..."

The King of Egret decided not to force Helgaia into any negotiations if they didn't feel comfortable opening themselves up to other nations. They were fine not to establish diplomatic ties, just so long as there wasn't any hostility. The king said that he wanted to honor Helgaia's wishes as much as possible.

Personally, I felt that they'd benefit from opening their borders a little bit like Xenoahs, but I agreed that forcing their hand wouldn't necessarily be good. I had a feeling the King of Egret felt the same, but he surely had his reasons.

"Now then... as for sending the pirates and the hostages back to Helgaia..."

The King of Egret glanced over to me. *Yep, no biggie.*

"I'll use [**Teleport**] to get to Helgaia, then I'll open a [**Gate**]. That's the safest way to do it."

I could've just warped there with Claudia and the others, but I didn't want to take any chances, since it was my first time moving toward Helgaia. I didn't want to end up in a bad spot.

"Thanks a lot, Grand Duke."

"Er... Huh?"

"The Grand Duke of Brunhild can use magic to move around. He can take you back to Helgaia in the blink of an eye!"

"Is such a thing really possible?"

The archfiend's bride stared at me in confusion. It must have seemed ludicrous to her, since she didn't live in a society with much magic. Plus, Helgaia was largely closed off to outsiders, so the idea of me just being able to appear there probably sounded odd.

"Alright, lemme just…"

"Your Highness!"

Totola Luphu, one of the king's attendants, came rushing into the room. I'd met him some time ago, back when he visited Brunhild on his giant bird.

"What's all the fuss about? You show disrespect to our guests."

"I apologize for my rudeness, but it's an emergency!"

"Huh? What's going on?"

"There are four black ships on the horizon! They're coming straight for us from the southwest!"

"What'd you say?!"

The King of Egret rose to his feet in a hurry. *More black ships? Is it more pirates? No, it's more likely to be…*

I opened up a [Gate] to the beach and headed there with the Claudia, her maids, and the king of Egret. I could see the silhouettes of four ships in the distance. They were still a fair bit away, but they were clearly the same kind of ship as the two we'd confiscated earlier.

"They were probably sent out in pursuit of the pirates."

"Mhm. Looks like I don't need to go to Helgaia anymore."

I nodded at the King of Egret, and Claudia placed a relieved hand over her chest. Elze, Hilde, and Yae, who had all been lounging on the beach, walked over.

"Are you going to go out and ask them to stop?"

"Pretty much, yeah. At the very least, I need to inform them that this is a country, and not some uninhabited area."

I sighed a little as I answered Hilde's question. I was getting a little tired of the chores…

Totola and the other Luphu riders could go out there and do it instead, but they'd be in trouble if they ended up getting fired upon.

"I just hope that the ship crews will be polite, I do."

"Same here. I really don't wanna dodge cannonballs again."

I used [Fly] for the second time that day, zoomed out toward the ships (keeping my distance this time), and triggered [Speaker].

"Attention, attention. Black ships, do you hear me? You are steadily approaching waters belonging to the Kingdom of Egret. Please stop your advance. If you're from Helgaia, please listen to what I'm saying. We have Lady Claudia, and she wishes for you to stop your advance as well."

Now all I had to do was wait and see.

The four ships moved forward for a little bit until the one at the front of the group started to slow its water wheels. The other three ships followed after that. It seemed they were complying with our requests. I slowly drew closer to the leading ship.

A pale-skinned man stood on the deck of the main ship. He had long, silver hair and wore a cape that fluttered in the breeze. He was staring right at me. The man was clearly vampiric. I could tell that at a glance. Which meant… he was probably the archfiend.

I landed on the deck. The demonkin around me regarded me with suspicious eyes. None of them raised their weapons, so I assumed a passive stance.

"Identify yourself. I am the Archfiend of Helgaia, Aluford Culhat Helgaia. In case it wasn't clear, I am a vampire lord."

Not just a regular vampire, huh? A vampire lord…

That reminded me, the overlord of Xenoahs had a vampire lord amongst the four elite ministers of his nation. That guy looked like he was in his twenties, but he was hundreds of years old.

"It's a pleasure to meet you, Archfiend. I am Mochizuki Touya. I preside over the Duchy of Brunhild as its Grand Duke. I hope we can get along."

My words caused the demonkin around me to murmur amongst themselves.

"A grand duke?"

"This kid is the king of that island?"

"But he said that island was Egret or whatever... What's the deal?"

"There's no way a world leader would come all the way out like this..."

Uh... Isn't your leader right here on the boat? He's standing right in front of me!

"Grand Duke of Brunhild, is my wife unharmed?"

Huh? Why's he glaring at me? I can sense a scary aura coming from him...

Apparently, I was the subject of a misunderstanding. They probably thought the pirates kidnapped Claudia on my orders.

"Sorry, let me just clear up something. The group of pirates that kidnapped your wife is completely unrelated to us. I recently rescued her and her maids, and they're currently settling in Egret's castle, completely safe and sound. I came out here to help return her to you."

The archfiend's expression changed into one of wide-eyed shock.

"...Oh, really? When they washed ashore, they kept saying that we wouldn't be forgiven by the outside world if we harmed them...

I assumed the kidnapping was some kind of plot from one of the human nations."

Nope, it was all a terrible coincidence. They just happened to break out as the queen was nearby. What a world.

I figured things would go faster if I had him meet with his wife, so I opened up a [Gate].

"Claudia!"

"Sweetheart!"

The archfiend rushed straight through the portal towards his wife on the beach, then gave her a tight hug. It was nice seeing such affection.

"Are you okay, my sweet? Are you harmed?"

"I'm okay. The Grand Duke of Brunhild saved me from those pirates, and the King of Egret has been more than welcoming."

Claudia smiled toward her husband, prompting the archfiend to look at the King of Egret.

"You're the leader of this land, then?"

"That I am. King of Egret, Lefang Letra. It's a pleasure to have you here in my nation."

"Thank you for your kindness. I truly appreciate the hospitality you've shown my wife. I cannot thank you enough."

"You'd be better off thanking my friend here. The Grand Duke of Brunhild saved Lady Claudia singlehandedly."

The archfiend stared at me in utter disbelief. It wasn't exactly singlehandedly... I had summoned two Krakens and a whole group of Merfolk to help.

"King of Egret, would you mind if I asked something...?"

"By all means."

"I admit we're not as worldly as other nations, but I hadn't noticed any nearby islands... Has... Has Egret always been here?"

"Ahaha. Don't worry, you should just ask the Grand Duke about that. He's a master manipulator of magic, with incredible knowledge about worldly events. He's also served as a mediator between many nations and led us toward prosperous relations. I'm sure he'll help you out."

Did you just volunteer me for the entire explanation?! I know I'm the most qualified guy, but still! Well, whatever. I'll just tell him about it. It's up to him if he believes me... And so, I projected a world map into the air with my smartphone.

"This is a current map of the world. Ever since that meteor shower a few days ago, two worlds were fused into one. The left half of the map is the world you'd be familiar with. The one on the right is the world I and the king of Egret are more familiar with."

"Really?! This is incredible... The two maps are identical, or rather, mirrored... Then, hold on... If this island here is Helgaia, then this one is..."

"Egret, yes. That's where we are right now." I then briefed the archfiend about the current situation with the mutants.

Apparently, no mutants had appeared in Helgaia. That was good, but also kind of a pain, since I had to explain a bit more about the threat they posed.

I played back a video of one of the fights we'd had against them, which allowed the archfiend to see the danger that could arise from one appearing in Helgaia.

"...I see. So, Grand Duke, you say you are trying to create a summit for the leaders of both worlds to meet?"

"Nothing too extreme, but yeah. I want us to negotiate and get along better, so all the nations can develop friendly relations."

I talked to him about the upcoming summit, which prompted him to ponder about it.

"Well, answer me this. In the world you know, how are fiends… How are people like me treated?"

"If I'm honest, well… There's still prejudice, and those that judge you on appearances. But most countries over here have laws against that kind of discrimination, and some nations accept demonkin unconditionally. We also have a nation similar to Helgaia. It's called Xenoahs."

"Oho… And what about… slavery?"

"Demonkin who commit crimes might be sentenced to hard labor in the mines, but that applies to humans as well, and most developed nations on our side have outright banned slavery in a non-penal context."

"I see…"

Only Yulong and Sandora recognized slavery as an everyday thing. Other countries only approved of slavery as a punishment for crime, and some nations didn't even allow that.

Given that Yulong and Sandora didn't really exist anymore, it was universally acknowledged that casual slavery just wasn't a thing anymore. Though obviously, there were underground slave trades and trafficking rings. We did make a habit of destroying those each time one was uncovered, though.

"Helgaia was formed as a result of human oppression. I'm sure many of my people would object to mixing with the outside world."

That was fair. Xenoahs was much the same. Even though they'd opened up borders, their scale was still small as far as trade went.

"But… Helgaia will have no future if it remains isolated. We'll slowly die as the rest of the world leaves us behind. As its leader, I must avoid that outcome."

"Then how about making ties with Egret to start? If your two countries established embassies in each other's territory, then you could help exchange culture."

After I spoke, the King of Egret took a step toward the archfiend.

"Mmh. If it's alright with you, Archfiend, I would like for Egret to extend a hand toward its new neighbors."

"...Very well. I think it would be a good first step. We'll be in your debt."

The archfiend shook hands with the king of Egret. I was glad to see things working out well there.

Obviously, I'd help out in bridging friendly relations between the two countries, as well. I told the archfiend to call on me if he needed help. In response to that, he glanced at his wife and then smiled in my direction.

"Actually... Enormous Tentaculars have started appearing in the seas around our country lately. They're disrupting the fishing trade... Do you perhaps have a solution for that?"

The king of Egret and I glanced at each other, and I let out a bitter chuckle.

Welp... Guess it's time for squid-fishing again.

It was finally the day of the multi-world summit.

Brunhild was the host country for the event, but obviously, that didn't mean much. All we did was provide the venue and help other countries set up anti-mutant countermeasures.

Also whenever countries had disputes, Brunhild would get called in to see if it could be resolved. My country was sort of like an arbiter nation at this point.

Just like during the days of the old alliance, the summit quickly turned into more of a party than anything else. We just let it happen at this point, since it was better if people had fun.

Various world leaders chatted and made merry with each other. It was nice to see.

There was no shortage of new and interesting people to talk to, since world leaders from the Reverse World territories were here as well.

The Reverse World nations we'd invited were:

The Kingdom of Primula.

The Triharan Holy Empire.

The Kingdom of Strain.

The Allent Theocracy.

The Gardio Empire.

The Lassei Military Kingdom.

The Kingdom of Panaches.

There were seven in total.

I asked the archfiend of Helgaia if he wanted to join in, but he elected to pass this time around. He was only interested in establishing firm relations with Egret as a first step.

I'd met with the rulers of Triharan, Strain, Primula, and Panaches before, but this was my first time talking to the leaders of Gardio, Allent, and Lassei.

The new Emperor of Gardio, Lancelet Rig Gardio, was a nice young man. After the whole situation with Isengard was over and Lucrecion stepped down as successor, the throne went to him instead.

We spoke a little bit, and I could tell he had serious and studious intent behind his eyes. Yumina confirmed his disposition with her mystic eye, saying he was pure of heart and determined. He was around the same age as Lestia's knight king and King Cloud of Lihnea. They all got to talking and seemed to become fast friends.

Next up came the Pontifex of Allent, Graud Zeth Allent.

He was close to sixty, but he didn't look that old at all. He was a large-framed man with an intense stare and a big white beard. He reminded me of Baba from Eashen in many ways.

Given that he was a holy leader, I imagined him as this slender and frail guy... But he ended up being a total macho man instead. Still, we had a beefy dude as the leader of Felsen, too.

Apparently, the Allent Theocracy was formed by a great hero who unified several tribes under the influence of various elemental spirits. The country then adopted a religion centered around the spirits, which were considered holy beings by the citizens of Allent.

When I explained to the Pontifex that I could use Spirit magic, he initially took offense. He declared, "You would dare to try and bend the holy spirits to your will?!" and other stuff like that.

After I explained to him that it wasn't like summoning, and that it was just reaching a mutual agreement with the spirits, he calmed down a bit and apologized.

Shirahime, the Mikado of Eashen, was also at the meeting. I brought the Pontifex to meet her, since she could summon the Snow Spirit (who also happened to be her mother). I could've summoned a spirit by myself, but I wanted to use the chance to bring some of the leaders closer together... Unfortunately, it didn't work out like I expected.

When Shirahime called the spirit out, the Pontifex immediately got down on all fours and started praying to her. Loudly. The Snow Spirit was so embarrassed and red in the face by this that she immediately returned to the spirit realm.

I couldn't blame the guy, since it was his first time ever seeing a spirit, but still... I promised him that I'd give him some elementary-level books about Spirit magic, which prompted him to grab me by the hands, and he thanked me profusely. His grip was so tight it hurt…

Still, everything was fine for the most part. Except for one world leader…

"I wish to fight Mochizuki Takeru! I've heard great things about your uncle!"

"I don't know about that…"

The sudden challenge came from the Grand Potentate of Lassei, Gimlet Gal Lassei.

He was Prince Zanbelt's father, and also one of the dragon clan, a dragonkin… Or, uh, a dragonewt.

He was a buff old guy. Kind of looked like a beefier, aged-up version of his kid, in fact. I could see multiple scars along his arms and neck.

Unfortunately for him, Takeru was away on a trip with Elze and Ende. He'd be back by the evening, but I didn't really want to have Lassei humiliated at an international summit.

"Didn't you hear what happened when your son tried to fight him?"

"I could tell at a glance that he thoroughly trounced my boy! Zanbelt's confidence was utterly broken, and he's been working far more earnestly as of late! I'd like to express my appreciation through combat with the man who helped my son."

"…That's kind of a weird leap in logic."

C'mon, man… At least be honest. You just want to fight, don't you? What a pain…

Moroha or Karina were available to fight him, but I really didn't want to humiliate the guy in front of everyone else. I grumbled quietly and wondered how to stop the guy asking when a ray of hope suddenly shone down from an unexpected source.

"If it's a bout you'd like, then why not face me, Grand Potentate?"

"Oh?"

The beastking of Mismede came wandering over with a smile on his face.

...Dude, really? Your own guards are burying their faces in their hands right now.

"You're the leader of Mismede..."

"Aye. I'm quite the fan of combat myself, and I feel like I could fight you without holding back. How about it?"

Wait, hold on here! Isn't this a little beyond normal socialization? This party was for us to chat, not fight...?

"Is there a good place for a battle?"

"The Brunhild knight order has a training field nearby. How about that?"

"Interesting. Sounds good to me!"

The Grand Potentate started to leave the room along with the beastking. They were both grinning madly.

"Wait, are you guys seriously gonna fight?!"

"Fret not, Touya my lad. I don't plan on holding any grudges if I lose. Plus, your training grounds are designed to prevent death, no?"

"Well, yeah... but..."

The training area had been set up to automatically cast [**Mega Heal**], [**Recovery**], and [**Refresh**] on anyone with sufficient injury. I set it up that way because I was worried Moroha would go too far while I was out of town or something. The knight king came to spar with her now and then, so it wouldn't exactly be a good look if my sister accidentally murdered the hell out of him one day.

...You know, come to think of it, inviting the king of Lestia over for Moroha to beat his ass isn't exactly good, either... So I guess

it's fine if these two spar? I grumbled a little bit, at which point the queen of Strain came over to tap me on the shoulder.

"Don't worry about it. The Grand Potentate is an honorable man. He would never mix personal grudge into political business."

I was still a bit worried, so I had Yae and Hilde go after them with orders to break any post-match spats up if it came down to it.

The Lassei and Mismede guards also followed after them, sighing heavily in unison. I felt bad for the regular soldiers assigned to guard those muscle-headed dorks.

"Oh, right. Have there been any Isengard refugees in Strain?"

Yumina suddenly spoke up, directing a question toward the Queen of Strain. I was actually interested in the answer to that as well. If my intel was correct, there were definitely a few people fleeing Isengard.

"Not as many as Gardio, but yes. But starting fresh in a new land is a difficult undertaking, so a lot of my people are worried the Isengardian refugees may turn to thievery or highway robbery."

It was a shame, but there was a high chance of that happening. Bastet and Anubis' intel suggested a lot of weird stuff was going on in Isengard.

I could understand wanting to flee such an uncertain country, but turning to crime in other countries just made the world worse. Refugees seemed to be an issue no matter the time or place... It certainly wasn't a big issue for the time being, but I knew it had the potential to become one.

"Do we know any more about what's happening in Isengard?"

"I've got people on it. Unless it's absolutely urgent, I'd suggest keeping as far away as possible. We need to take a lot of care when dealing with them right now."

"Why? Do you think Isengard could launch an invasion?"

"Not Isengard, no... But there could definitely be a fight."

I was certain that the mutant Dominant Constructs were behind this. I was only aware of a handful. There was Yula, the one that helped form the wicked god. Then, there were the twins, Leto and Luto, the ones that roughed up Ende. I knew about those three, but there could've still been more. I needed to talk more about this with the Sovereign Phrase, Melle, as well as Ney. They probably had more information about the Phrase in general.

"Are there any issues in your world right now? Er, rather... on your continent? Any strange incidents or conflicts?"

"Conflicts, hm... Zadonia, the land of ice, has recently stepped up its conflict against Dauburn, the land of fire."

If I recalled correctly, Zadonia and Dauburn were two nations to the north of Allent. I'd heard a bit about their conflicts before.

"Those countries fight like cats and dogs. If Zadonia brings up a point, then Dauburn will immediately double down on that point being wrong. If Dauburn imports a specific model of Gollem, then Zadonia will import slightly more of the same Gollem out of spite. It's almost a tradition at this point for them to feud and one-up each other."

Fighting like cats and dogs, huh? Reminds me of some nations back on Earth.

"Zadonia's environment is covered in ice and snow, while Dauburn's is a heat-ridden desert. They have polar opposite environments, despite their close proximity. Apparently, the royal families of each nation pass down a story blaming the other country for their habitat."

"Huh? A story? Don't they know the actual reasons?"

"I don't believe so. I only know the stories mention something was stolen."

"Stolen by who?"

"Both sides."

That sounded odd to me. I asked for a little more information, and apparently both oral traditions claimed that the other country stole something of great value. I couldn't really say I understood.

The Pontifex of Allent was more knowledgeable about this stuff, so I asked him.

"Ah, that tale. I hear the old scrolls of Zadonia and Dauburn state that Zadonia was cursed by an ice goddess, while Dauburn was cursed by a fire demon. Apparently, both sides stole offerings from the other, incurring the wrath of both entities. From what we understand, at least... Dauburn stole Zadonia's offering to the ice goddess, while Zadonia stole Dauburn's offering to the fire demon..."

Hrmm... So... Dauburn was offering something to a fire demon, and Zadonia was offering something to an ice goddess... and they stole each other's offerings? Then the goddess and the demon caused the harsh environments as retribution? Hrmm... I don't really think it was a real god or a real demon, though. I mean, gods aren't even allowed to interfere in stuff like this.

The incident at the Ramissh Theocracy sprang to mind, and I wondered if this was another case of spirits causing trouble. "What are you pondering, Grand Duke? Are you perhaps thinking of bringing Zadonia and Dauburn together? Even if you are our global conciliator, that would be quite the tall order. Those two tend not to take the advice of others."

The pontifex commented all of a sudden. *Uhhh... global conciliator? When did I get that job?*

"Then again, you did bring Primula and Triharan together. You even stopped the war between Gardio and Isengard. Maybe you could do it!"

"Ah, those incidents weren't exactly planned, I just…"

The King of Primula must have overheard our conversation, since he walked over and started to talk.

"I was a little surprised when you kidnapped the Triharan commander, Touya. Are you perhaps planning on kidnapping the leaders of Zadonia and Dauburn as well?"

"No, absolutely not! Please don't make out like I'm some kind of serial kidnapper… Though it might be good to get them into a secluded space where they can talk to each other like adults and leaders."

"I have my doubts about that. They'd be more likely to start beating each other to a pulp."

…That doesn't sound good. Maybe it'd be better if I tied them up with rope? Ugh, now I really am sounding like a seasoned kidnapper.

If there was some kind of personal grudge, I'd be fine with letting them deal with it, but I didn't exactly want them causing trouble for their people.

"Do the people of both countries hate the other side, too?"

"Not the commoners, at least. I'm fairly sure most of them would be happy if the grudge match ended. After all, the rivalry means orders like forced conscription are in place. Most able-bodied people in both countries are called to war at least once a year for some petty grudge fight, and I can't imagine they like it. Nobody can live near the borders, either. Every time they have one of their yearly wars, the territory shifts slightly."

Apparently, even if one side won the battle, they'd immediately retreat because they couldn't handle the harsh climate of their won land. What a bunch of morons.

"In truth, we Allentese people are quite content with their constant feuding. It means neither country will ever try and quarrel with us."

It seemed like if either Zadonia or Dauburn attacked Allent, that would leave them open targets to their most hated rivals. Neither Panaches nor the Kingdom of Gem had been attacked by those nations, either.

From that perspective, letting the two countries constantly bicker could potentially be good for world peace. But then I glanced around the room and saw the king of Lihnea laughing alongside the young king of Palouf, which made me immediately change my mind.

Palouf and Lihnea had similar skirmishes against each other for many years, too. That was largely because Prime Minister Wardack had taken control of Lihnea, and he was planning on messing the whole place up with that crappy fake prince, Zabune. After all that was settled, the two nations gradually made peace. Hell, now Princess Lucienne of Palouf was even engaged to King Cloud of Lihnea. It was a great union.

If any countries were proof that relations could be repaired, Lihnea and Palouf were prime examples. It also helped that both Lihnea and Palouf had their leaders changed, though…

I decided to keep an eye on Dauburn and Zadonia before deciding to do anything. I didn't want to become a proactive meddler in international affairs.

As I thought quietly to myself, my phone began vibrating against my chest pocket. It was a call from Guildmaster Relisha.

Oh, she must be calling to see if I got permission to set up guilds on the reverse continent. I was planning on bringing that up during the afterparty, but it seems like we're in full-on party mode right now, anyway...

I quickly picked up the call.

"Heyo, what's up?"

"It's Relisha. We've detected an upcoming mutant emergence zone."

"...Where?"

"It's... in the sea... Or above the sea. Hard to say. Either way, it's in the waters between Refreese, Lihnea, and Panaches. We can't tell where the emergence point is exactly, but it's around there."

The sea? Seriously? That's never happened before. If it was just regular Phrase coming out, we'd be able to predict where they'd go, since they only targeted humans in a mechanical way. But the mutants are way more erratic.

They probably had some kind of goal, though. They wouldn't come out for no reason. But whether that goal was to serve the wicked god's plan, or some whim of the mutated Dominant Constructs remained to be seen. All we could do for the time being was observe them and figure out their target.

The only saving grace to this situation was that there were no innocent human settlements out at sea.

"How many can we expect, and when?"

"Roughly ten-thousand. We're getting similar readings to the emergence event at Yulong. We estimate they'll break through in roughly thirty hours."

Almost the same amount as the Yulong invasion... All of them are mutants too, geez. But still, we're much stronger and far more unified now. I have Reginleif, and all my fiancees have their personal frame gears. We've got new models for the Chevaliers and Knight Barons, and we even have two brand new Over Gears.

I'm not worried about this fight. I have the backing of most of the countries in this new, unified world. Nothing can possibly go wrong.

I told the leaders present at the summit about the incoming mutant invasion and asked them to nominate knights to participate in the defensive battle.

No way in hell I'm letting these mutants or that wicked god just do as they please. This is our world, not theirs.

I lent twenty Frame Gears to each participating nation. Two Knight Barons and eighteen Chevaliers.

Just about every country in the regular world... I mean, the eastern continent, was participating. Excluding Brunhild, there were eighteen participants in total. The tribes from the Sea of Trees weren't participating because they were so prideful when it came to their physical prowess that they refused to battle inside Frame Gears. Twenty Frame Gears to each of the eighteen countries made for a total of three-hundred-and-sixty Frame Gears. Then, there were fifty being deployed by Brunhild, plus my Reginleif and the nine Valkyrie gears. In total, there were four-hundred-and-twenty mechs ready for combat.

When Yulong was invaded, we only had two-hundred Frame Gears, so now we had more than twice that. We definitely had the advantage, but we needed to keep in mind that the mutants were trickier than regular Phrase. We couldn't make light of them.

Norn and Nia were also here in their Over Gears. I also made Ende come along with his Dragoon. Our forces were completely prepared, there was just one issue...

"They're actually emerging in the middle of the sea, huh...?" Doctor Babylon grumbled as she crossed her arms. She was surveying a map on one of her laboratory monitors.

"How waterproof are our Frame Gears right now?"

"Reginleif and the Valkyries will be fine, same with the Over Gears and Ende's Dragoon. Even if you fully submerge there shouldn't be any issues... Though you should expect slower reaction times thanks to water resistance. The other Frame Gears are a no-go, though. Their cockpits don't have appropriate sealing measures. They'll be fine up to their waists, but any deeper and they'll start taking on water. It could easily endanger the pilots if it comes to that."

In a worst-case scenario, our pilots could end up drowned... There was always the emergency escape button, though, so I didn't think it'd be likely for anyone to actually drown. That being said, someone could fall unconscious and then have their Frame Gear submerged, which would be certain death. It was definitely safer to fight on the land.

"We still don't know what they'll do... Our best bet is to monitor them with search magic after they emerge, then set up defenses in their path."

"Don't forget there'll probably be airborne ones as well." We had a few ways of dealing with flying enemies. Reginleif and Helmwige were capable of flying. Brunnhilde, Grimgerde, Rossweisse, and Waltraute (with its cannon equipped) were capable of long-distance assaults, too. I was sure we'd be fine.

I left the fine-tuning of the remaining Frame Gears to Babylon and her workers, then I left for Brunhild castle. I happened to see Karen nearby, so I walked over to ask something I'd been worried about.

"You wanna know if the enemy'll use divine venom?"

"Yeah. If they started spreading it around, then I wouldn't be able to participate. Neither would Yumina and the others."

"Don't worry about that, you know? Divine venom is soaked into the earth and air. It basically turns a vast area into an anti-divine zone, you know? But I mentioned earlier that the venom doesn't mix well with water. The seawater should dilute it and disperse it before it can do any real damage, you know? Plus, it's a hard substance to create to begin with."

That meant the meteor shower might have depleted their current supply of the stuff.

"Divine venom is created by sacrificing the soul of a god, you know? So we probably have a good idea of what was used to create this batch…"

"…The servile god who got eaten, huh?"

That annoying NEET god had his body absorbed, and now his soul was being used to create poison… What a hopeless idiot. He really did get what was coming to him.

I guess you could consider the divine venom coating Isengard some kind of last curse from that NEET bastard. Why does that asshole have to cause me trouble from beyond the grave? What was he the god of again? Being a total annoying sack of crap?

"Still, we need to keep thinking up ways to counteract the divine venom… Have you guys been working on anything?"

"The god of agriculture, er, Kousuke is attempting to cultivate a plant that can absorb the venom and convert it into magic energy. It isn't going well though, you know?"

"Is it a hard job?"

"I'll say. He's basically trying to infuse his divinity to create a whole new species linked to him from scratch, you know? It's even more complex than forming elemental spirits."

That definitely sounded tough. That also explained why I hadn't seen Uncle Kousuke around very much… I made a mental note to visit him with some snacks later on.

Just as I was thinking about what he might like, my phone started vibrating. It was a call from Ende.

"Hey, what's up?"

"Hey, Touya? Sorry but there's something I wanna discuss. Could you come over?"

"To your house?"

"Yup."

Ende, Melle, Ney, and Lycee lived together in a house in the castle town. It wasn't too far from the castle, so I decided to walk over.

On the way there I looked north from the terrace to the training field. Rosetta was over there making final adjustments to the Over Gears.

I could see the prone figures of the two massive mechanical animals, one red and one black. The two Over Gears certainly looked impressive from a distance. And so, I headed a little closer and saw the irritatingly familiar image of a certain pumpkin-pantsed prince.

"What brings you here…?"

"Ah, Touya! Most impeccable timing! I never would've expected the crown's abilities could be used in this way!" Robert was practically swooning at the sight of the two Over Gears.

…*This bastard came here with Blau's ability, didn't he? Come on, man… I have it bad enough with Karen and the other divines popping up out of nowhere.*

"Nia! Norn! May I ride in that too?! Please! Pretty, pretty please!"

"Shut the hell up, sleepy!"

"You should stick to babbling in your sleep. It's annoying for you to do it awake as well."

Robert stepped a little closer and took an iron claw attack from Nia and a shin kick from Norn. He was certainly as irksome as ever, but that was basically this guy's default state of being.

"Over Gears are attuned to the Gollems inside them, so only that Gollem's master can pilot them. Even if you boarded either of these, they wouldn't move."

"Ah, really?!"

"They're pretty much exclusive to crown Gollems anyway. Norn's Leo Noir and Nia's Tiger Rouge were the same Over Gear structurally, but we couldn't swap the Gollems operating at the heart of either. We do have another spare frame for parts and stuff, but we don't have a crown to make use of it…"

I suddenly covered my mouth, realizing the fatal mistake I'd just made. Robert's glittering gaze pierced through my very soul. *Ugh… I don't really like being looked at like this by a guy…*

"So you're saying you could make one of these machines for my crown, Blau?! I can have one to ride in as well? Oh, that's amazing, Touya! Thank you so much!"

"N-Now hold on a second… That's not so simple…"

"You should just build it already, dumbass. That pesky prince'll just keep bugging you daily until it's finished."

Damn it.

Norn's words felt like they came from her own experience. I cast a glance toward Rosetta, who responded with a sigh.

"Well, sir! The base is fundamentally identical, so we could make one. Yessir we can! But it'd take a while to tune up and synchronize with his Gollem, sir!"

"Norn has a lion, and Nia has a tiger… I wonder what I should have! Perhaps a magnificent deer! Although, if you two have cat-based models, perhaps a dog? Oh, perhaps a wolf or a fox! What do you two think?"

"I can't really say I give a crap one way or another. Maybe a blobfish? That'd suit your face."

"Bear sounds good to me. Why don't you make like one and hibernate forever?"

Robert was seemingly unaffected by the girls and their harsh words. I was pretty impressed by his mental fortitude...

"We won't be able to make you one in time for the upcoming battle. You'll be with the other western world leaders, observing the fight."

"Hrmm... What a shame! Well, I'll simply participate next time, then. Do you think you'll be alright without my power, though? I must admit, I worry a little that you only have Norn and Nia!"

"Huh? You trying to start a fight with me, idiot?"

"You're the last person I want to hear being worried about me."

Robert took another iron claw to the face from Nia, then another shin-kick from Norn. He did actually seem genuinely concerned for them, he just didn't speak with much tact...

The ultra-masochistic prince cheerily ate all punishments the girls had to offer.

Welp, I'm sticking around too long. Better head off... I left Robert and the others behind and made my way to the castle town.

After a while, I walked through the garden in front of the large house near the castle town's outskirts. Melle, who looked human thanks to my magic device, came out to greet me.

"Ahhh, Touya. Welcome to our home. It's been a little while."

Even though she had the appearance of a regular girl, she still looked like the Sovereign Phrase to me. She was wearing an apron, and almost gave off the image of a young and happy housewife. I was suddenly filled with the urge to punch Ende in the face.

I entered the house. It was a good size, but it wasn't overly fancy or anything. Ende, Lycee, and Ney were waiting for me inside.

It wasn't polite of me to show up without a gift, so I opened up [Storage] and gave some cookies to Lycee.

"Sorry to bother you. There was just something I wanted to discuss."

"What's up? Is it something to do with the battle?"

I sipped some tea as I spoke with Ende. I'd asked him to participate in the fight with his Dragoon, so I was wondering if he had some kind of issue with that.

"That's part of it, at least. Melle and the other Dominant Constructs can sense traces of the mutants, since they were formerly kin. They can sense them when they try to emerge from the space between worlds. They can't tell timing and numbers as well as the guild's sensors, but there are actually areas where they're better."

"How so?"

"They can identify the construct classes that are coming through. There are going to be Upper Constructs during the battle tomorrow. But that's not the main thing here... They sensed that Dominant Constructs are going to come through as well."

"What?!"

A mutant Dominant...

The Phrase were originally split into two factions. Ney's side, who wanted to find Melle... and Yula's side, who wanted to find other means of power. In the end, most of the Phrase got consumed by Yula's mutant army and became fodder for the wicked god. Ney ended up reuniting with Melle, and joined our side.

"If the Dominant Constructs that appear end up being Leto and Luto, can you let me handle them? I have a score to settle."

"Leto and Luto, huh...? Those were the twins who roughed you up so hard you ran off crying, right?"

"Crying?! Hey! I might have run off, but I wasn't crying!"

"I dunno, man... You seemed pretty desperate to me. You went to another world and got some sacred treasure blades, then Uncle Takeru beat your ass so bad you lost your memories and ended up being used as a pawn by the corrupt nobility of Triharan... Remember?"

"Auuugh! Shut up! Shut uuup!" Ende closed his eyes and shook his head violently, prompting Ney to smack him in the side of the head.

"You're the one who should shut up, loudmouth!"

"Gagh!"

Ende slumped down against the couch.

"I have a score to settle with Leto and Luto, too. Mind letting us do it?"

"I'm fine with it, so long as you don't have an issue with me stepping in if it gets too bad."

"Thank you. I appreciate it."

Ney bowed her head slightly. She'd certainly softened up a bit after settling in Brunhild... She used to be the kind of person who felt like she'd bite your head off. Seemed like Melle and the others had a calming influence.

It made sense, though. Her goal was always to reunite with Melle.

"Actually, I've been meaning to ask. How many Dominant Constructs are with the mutants?"

"Back before the golden corruption, it was only Luto, Leto, Yula, and Gila against me. But I don't know if the situation has changed."

"How do you mean?"

I quirked a brow in response to Ney's words. I'd beat Gila so that would only mean three of them remained…

"We came searching for Lady Melle, the sovereign. But it's possible that Yula called more Dominants from Phrasia. He'd been planning to usurp Lady Melle for a long time, since before we started traveling through worlds. I'd be surprised if he didn't have more Dominants on his side."

And if those Dominants became mutants… Let's face it, they definitely would, then they'd probably end up joining the upcoming invasion force.

If the emerging Dominants weren't Leto and Luto, then I planned on having Moroha, Takeru, and Karina take them on. In times like this, it was best to turn to the gods for help… Even if I was a god myself, I was a trainee! They had a job to support me!

"Oh, right… Ende, do you think you can beat mutant Dominant Constructs?"

"Hey… Don't think so lightly of me. I'm a disciple of the god of combat himself, right? Ahaha… Do you know how many times I've faced death in that hellish training? Ahaha… Ahhh… Y-You have no idea what I've faced… M-My mind is clear, my heart is pure… Ahaha… Ahahahahaaaah… Augh…"

I didn't know what Ende was recalling, but his eyes swirled around in his head, and he began to laugh bitterly. I honestly worried about his health sometimes...

"Get it together, Endymion."

"Ack. Y-Yes, I'm fine. Thank you, Melle. I was just thinking about my training."

Melle shook Ende a little, and he returned to normal. I wondered if Takeru wasn't going a little far with the training. Frankly, I didn't want Elze to turn out like this guy, so I was a little worried about her.

"...Thanks for the snacks."

I was wondering why Lycee hadn't said anything during my entire visit. That mystery was answered when I looked at her and saw the entire bag of cookies was gone. She certainly operated on her own wavelength...

...Are we gonna be fine tomorrow? No, I'm sure we will be. We've prepared everything we possibly can, now all that's left is to crush the enemy.

We've got new allies with us... They'll probably help. Probably. It's definitely gonna be fine.

Probably. I think.

"They're coming."

Markers began falling down all over the place on my map. Upper Constructs needed more time to get through, so the markers all represented Lesser and Intermediate Constructs.

The Dominant Constructs would take time to come out as well... The ideal situation would be to mop up all the mooks before the real threats showed up.

"How annoying… Wish they'd just appeared in front of us."

I could hear Elze's annoyed voice come out from Reginleif's cockpit comms. I understood her feelings.

I looked at the emergence zone with a divinity-infused [**Long Sense**] spell, but I could only see flying mutants.

Given my map's markers, the rest were probably crawling along the seafloor.

"They're headed directly southwest, then… Seems like Yumina's prediction was entirely correct."

"Yup. That's probably the case."

Hilde was on the mark. Before the mutants had shown up, Yumina suggested that the mutants might have been trying to make a beeline for Isengard.

Just as she'd said, that was exactly the direction in which they were headed. And that meant they'd have to pass by Panaches first.

I'd already received permission from the king of Panaches to deploy soldiers to his territory. I'd summoned several Valkyries to record the battle, which was being transmitted to a live feed back at the Brunhild HQ.

All the leaders of the east and west continents would be watching that screen, the King of Panaches included.

I had four-hundred-and-twenty Frame Gears lining the Panaches coastline.

All of them stared out to sea, waiting for their enemy to appear.

If it was any other terrain, I'd have used [**Meteor Rain**] to trash a bunch of them, but I held back due to fears of causing a tsunami.

"Touya, are we cleared to deploy against the flying ones?"

"Think so… Yeah, we are."

I gestured up toward Linze's Helmwige. It was in flight mode, ready at my command.

The only two Frame Gears that had flight-based capabilities by default were my Reginleif and Linze's Helmwige. Rosetta had, however, engineered several flying packs for the Valkyrie gears. Yae's Schwertleite and Hilde's Siegrune had both used them in the past. But unfortunately, we realized that they put too much strain on the pilot and the machines, so we had Doctor Babylon go back to the drawing board... She didn't design anything in time for this fight, though. The Over Gears had taken priority.

To be honest, having flying attachments was a pretty niche and situational requirement anyway. If the enemy didn't show up above the sea, then Brunnhilde's sniping, Grimgerde's barrage, and Rossweisse's waveform attacks would've been more than enough to deal with airborne foes.

I had Reginleif float upward and stop level with Helmwige.

"Linze, stay within Brunnhilde's firing radius. Yumina, support Linze with your sniper."

"One shot, one kill. I'll handle this."

I was more than comfortable leaving that side of things in Yumina's hands.

Reginleif soared through the air. Though the sea's surface was calm, I knew that beneath the waves, an army of mutated monsters was coming for us. There were roughly a thousand airborne mutants headed our way like a flock of birds as well.

"Fragarachs activate! Mode Change: Dagger!"

The twelve wing-esque crystal slabs on Reginleif's back immediately shifted into forty-eight tiny daggers. Then, they began orbiting the mech.

"Let's go! [**Gladius**]!"

The forty-eight orbiting blades shimmered in the sunlight, rushing headlong toward the inbound flying foes.

I used my divine sight to verify the locations of the cores and pierced through them precisely. The crystal blades danced through the air, leaving a glimmering trail behind them as they cut mutant after mutant. The creatures melted down into goop and faded into the sea.

The mental strain behind that attack was rough, though... Manipulating forty-eight blades at once, even with the boosted mental capacity from [**Accel**], was a difficult task.

Linze's Helmwige masterfully took down the ones that slipped through the cracks of my attack. The two revolver cannons on her wings automatically sought out enemies and pummeled them with crystal projectiles.

Just like Leen's Grimgerde, it didn't run out of ammo. We had them set up to automatically reload via teleportation from Babylon's ammo stores.

Still, if we had revolver cannons on all our Frame Gears, we'd definitely run out of ammunition too quickly. Plus, it increased the risk of friendly fire.

Yumina's sniper shots took the ones Linze and I missed every now and then. True to her word, she was capable of firing through the core of each one with just a single shot.

Her aim was incredible, especially since she didn't have divine sight. I wondered if she was using her foresight ability to assist her aim... Maybe she saw the images of the future and knew exactly where to hit. Thanks to Linze and Yumina, I'd already taken out more than half the flying enemies.

I checked the radar map in my cockpit, and the mutants on the seabed were still marching toward the Panaches shoreline. They'd already moved beneath us, so I decided it was best to worry about dealing with the flying ones.

I used [**Gladius**] to melt more and more of the mutants. And eventually, their numbers were thinned to a quarter of the original amount.

"Touya! They're making landfall now!"

I heard Sue's voice through the speaker and turned the camera feed toward the beach. A vast swarm of coconut crabs, crawfish, and other crustacean-shaped mutants emerged from the depths. The filthy constructs scuttled along the beach, exuding a murky golden glow as they marched onward. I saw a few isopods and regular crab-shaped ones, too.

"Looks like our guests have arrived. Time to roll out the welcome wagon!"

Leen and Paula were inside Grimgerde's cockpit, weapons primed. Various segments on the black Frame Gear's body began opening up. Arms, chest, legs, and waist... all opened, exposing Gatling cannons and pod missiles.

"Get blasted, sea scum!"

A hail... Or rather, a total storm of crystal bullets crashed down upon the landborne mutants. Countless enemies were reduced to barely recognizable shapes, utterly obliterated by the barrage.

"Wow! Let me give it a go, too!"

Sue's Ortlinde Overlord raised its right arm high into the sky. I knew what was coming next...

"Cannon Knuckle Spiral!"

The powerful rocket-powered punch slammed into a group of mutants, mowing them down with ease. The arm wasn't stopping there, though. It skidded across the beach and plunged into the sea, kicking up sand and saltwater all over the place.

The rocket-punch continued mowing through submerged enemies until it eventually broke the surface and created a vast pillar of water in its wake. That attack was seriously strong...

Sue's Frame Gear really wasn't suited for combat against fodder.

"Let us roll, let us!"

"Yeah."

"Let's do this!"

Yae's Schwertleite, Hilde's Siegrune, and Elze's Gerhilde charged out onto the beach. The Frame Gears behind them, piloted by soldiers from all around the eastern continent, took up their arms and charged as well.

"I'll support you from behind!"

Lu's Waltraute swapped out to its C-Unit and began swiftly supporting the others across the battlefield.

The C-Unit was a long-range cannon on the right shoulder, allowing Lu to snipe the enemies one after the other.

Music began blaring from Rossweisse's speakers.

...This song of all things. I don't imagine Sakura'll have a satisfying answer if I ask her why she chose this one.

It was a song by a famous rock band from England. Specifically, it was by their lead vocalist. His band members arranged this version and had it released after he died of illness at forty-five years old. I had the original release, too.

The lyrics were direct and to the point, with lines like, "I was born to love you." The lead singer's voice was powerful enough to shake anyone down to the soul.

Sakura's voice rang out across the battlefield, just as clearly and powerfully as the original singer's voice. The soundwaves reverberated against the ether liquid inside the Frame Gears, giving them temporary boosts.

"Brunhild knights, charge!"

"Belfast knights, move out!"

"Don't hold back, Regulus knights! Show them that we're a force to be reckoned with!"

The knights began to clash against the mutants as the battle music invigorated them. Steel clashed against muddied gold, smashing the Lesser Constructs to bits. Then, they began tactically surrounding the Intermediate Constructs as well.

The ground was littered with smashed cores and black sludge. It was a little late to think about, but I hoped this wouldn't pollute the sea at all. I was kind of worried this would turn into an oil tanker spill situation or something. The waters looked mostly okay, though, so I figured it was probably fine.

"Oh?"

I looked over to the beach and saw two mechanical animals charging around the mutant horde. It was almost as if they were competing.

The two Over Gears emitted shockwaves that prevented the mutants from even approaching them. The enemies were blasted over by the shockwaves, allowing the knights to rush in and stab them while they were down.

At a glance, it seemed like a clever, coordinated attack. But I knew better. They were just charging around as they pleased.

"Hey, Over Gears. Don't go charging into our allies, okay?"

"Hey, geez. You think I'd do something like that? Trust me here."

"Don't get too ahead of yourself now. You're the kinda person who charges in without thinking."

"Excuse me?!"

I sighed slightly as the two started bickering over the comms. But thankfully, a shining goddess appeared to save me.

"Nia… I'm fairly sure I'm always telling you not to charge on blindly."

"Est?! H-Huh?! Why are you here?!"

The deputy leader of the Red Cats, Est, appeared behind Nia in her Red Lynx Frame Gear.

"I didn't invite the Red Cats to participate this time around, but I let Est deploy with our knight order. I needed someone to keep you in check, after all."

"Jerk!"

"Now, now. Enough of that. I thought you'd be fine left to your own devices, but it seems like I really do have to tug at your reins…"

Est's Red Lynx deftly leaped into the air and straddled Tiger Rouge. Seemed like when she said that stuff about rein-tugging, she meant it literally.

"Now, then. Hi-ho, Nia! Away!"

"I'm not a horse!"

"There's nothing wrong with being a horse. Now, let's work hard together… Unless you don't want dinner, that is."

"Augh!"

Tiger Rouge rode out along the shore with Red Lynx on its back. They were fighting pretty well together. It really spoke to their history.

The battle was slowly becoming more of an all-out brawl, but we clearly had the upper hand. Brunnhilde and Waltraute were doing a great job of supporting the less experienced pilots.

I suddenly received a message from Ende's Dragoon.

"Touya, Upper Constructs inbound. Melle says there are three of them."

"What?!"

Three… This wasn't the first time multiple big ones had shown up. I remembered the incident with the nautilus and the peacock.

Come to think of it, that was the first time we ever saw mutated Upper Constructs.

Three of them would be a struggle, though... Especially with Dominant Constructs coming in after them.

"Touya, look at the sea!"

I turned in response to Yumina's voice and saw an enormous whirlpool forming nearby. *Wait, the Upper Constructs are showing up here instead of with the Lesser ones?!*

The whirlpool kept on growing larger until it resembled an antlion's nest made of water.

Eventually, the middle of that whirlpool began to fracture, and space itself started cracking.

The cracking spread to the left and right and reality at the center of the whirlpool shattered like a mirror. The whirlpool vanished, replaced by three massive creatures above the sea.

"Incoming!"

The first one came crashing down into the water. It stood up on its hind legs as if to intimidate us. It was small for an Upper Construct and had the shape of a stag beetle.

That still didn't mean it was small by human standards. It was about as tall as an office building. I had a feeling even our Frame Gears could be crushed up in its mandibles.

The second one floated on the sea's surface. It had a star-like shape... It was clearly some kind of starfish. It slowly rotated as it floated along the water.

It was over a hundred meters long, at least as wide as a baseball stadium.

The final one that pushed itself through space and appeared before us was... A Dragon.

It was a two-headed Dragon.

It had the physical appearance of a western Dragon, the kind of bulky fire-breathing monster you'd see in stories of knights and chivalry. This one didn't have any wings, though.

Spikes jutted out from its body from head to tail. It even had gnarled horns sticking out of its chest.

The worst thing about it was its size, though. It had to have been at least one and a half times as large as the starfish. This was absolutely the largest Upper Construct I'd ever seen.

The two-headed Dragon splashed down into the water, all four of its clawed feet digging into the seabed. Water splashed all over the place.

It was only then that I noticed the figures standing atop the Dragon's heads. Two Dominant Constructs with muddy-gold protrusions on their bodies. They almost looked like identical twins, but one was male and the other female. They weren't very tall, either. They didn't give off the vibe of a man or a woman. Instead, they were more like a boy and a girl.

Two Dominant Constructs with similar appearances... Don't tell me that's...

"Touya, you promised, remember?"

I heard Ende's voice on the comms.

"So that means they're who I think they are?"

"That's right. Leto and Luto. The ones that caused the whole mess for me a while back."

I looked back up toward the Dragon and saw the twin mutants cackling atop the heads.

"It would appear we have a great many spectators, Luto. Whatever shall we do?"

"We must greet our new friends with open arms, of course."

The two-headed Dragon dug its feet into the seabed even more as it aimed its heads at the shoreline. Crackling electricity began to dance all over its body as particles of light gathered in both of its open mouths.

OH HELL NO! Two enormous lasers beamed from the Dragon's mouths in the blink of an eye, sending out a burning flash of light into the vicinity.

"[Shield]!"

I cast a defensive spell, empowered by my own divinity and Reginleif. Usually, the barrier was invisible, but it glowed with divine light as it stood in the path of the two particle beams.

In most cases, a spell imbued with divinity was unbreakable, but since the enemy was empowered by the wicked god, the circumstances were far from normal. The barrier I'd set up gradually began to crack and strain under the force of the incoming blasts.

Fortunately, it managed to endure the full brunt of the attack, but it shattered to pieces right after.

"Way to attack hard right off the bat, geez…"

I was a little worried for a second there. I hadn't expected them to do that.

"Hey, Ende. I'm gonna move these two someplace else. You good to take them after that?"

"Yeah. You can leave it to me, Melle, and the others."

"Gotcha. Let me just set that up for you then. Fragarach Mode Change: Chain!"

The forty-eight daggers orbiting Reginleif joined together and formed chain links, then combined into a single large chain. Both ends of the chain had weighty phrasium ball weights attached to them.

The chain, imbued with my divinity, orbited Reginleif as it gradually lengthened.

"Go now. Snare those two Dominant Constructs, Gleipnir!"

The phrasium chain hurtled toward Leto and Luto at incredible speed, wrapping itself around them like a crystal snake.

"What is this?!"

"How is this…?!"

The two ball weights dragged down as the chains bound Leto and Luto, drawing them both together.

I knew it wouldn't last long, so I deftly sent the two of them blasting toward a sand dune away from the main battle.

"Gh!"

The chains around the duo started to crack under their resistance. Given that they had the wicked god's muddy divinity, I wasn't surprised.

I didn't want the Fragarachs breaking this soon into the fight, so I released them from their bonds, dropping them to the sand below.

The two of them landed without issue, but it wasn't over for them.

"[Prison]!"

I used my sealing spell to lock them up. Under ordinary circumstances, they wouldn't have been able to escape.

Unfortunately for me, I was pretty sure that if they focused their attacks, they'd be able to get out at some point.

Well, if they could focus, anyway.

"They're confined to that area. Do what you want with them now."

"Cheers, Touya."

The black-and-white Dragoon sped toward the dune, holding Melle and the other two Phrase girls in its hands.

The Dragoon came to a halt and they all leaped down to the ground. Then, Ende popped open his cockpit and joined them.

"Hoh. And here I was wondering what this was all about. Are you not the former sovereign and her ragtag gang of weaklings?"

"Goodness me, Ney? I never would have imagined you teaming up with Endymion of all people. I was sure you ran back to Phrasia in tears, tail between your legs like the good little dog you are."

Ende and his allies walked through the [**Prison**] threshold, ignoring the jeering from the twins. I'd set it up so anything other than the mutants could pass through it.

"...Leto. Luto. It's been a while, hasn't it?" Melle called out to the twins as she and her allies stood to face them.

I was a bit worried about how they'd fare, but I decided to trust in them. I had a lot to do, after all.

I transformed the Fragarach chain links back into flat boards and had them rest on Reginleif's back. We had to deal with the incoming Upper Constructs.

"Touya, how shall we handle them?"

I didn't reply to Yumina for a few moments, since I was contemplating our course of action.

"Sue, deploy your Overlord against the stag beetle. Sakura, you support her. Yae, Elze, and Hilde, take Linze with you and target the starfish. Leen, Lu, and Yumina... You cover the knights and attack the Upper Constructs when you have an opportunity. I'll handle that two-headed Dragon. If you guys take down your target, immediately go and back up the other girls."

The stag beetle was seventy or eighty meters long at most and Sue's Ortlinde Overlord was thirty meters, so I was sure it could hold back the beetle if it came down to it.

Ortlinde had been designed from the ground-up as a defensive Frame Gear anyway. It had impeccable defenses. If you added in Sakura's music as support, they'd be unstoppable.

I was a bit concerned about the starfish, since I didn't know how it would attack, but I had faith in the four girls I'd sent after it.

All I had to do was take out the two-headed Dragon as quickly as I could, then help the others as needed.

I'm counting on you, Ende. Don't let those Dominant Constructs get over here.

"Valkyries, move out!"

I reactivated the Fragarachs on Reginleif's back, then flew off toward my target.

"Alright, now it's our turn!"

Sue sat inside the Ortlinde Overlord's cockpit. She was positively brimming with joy. She was excited to finally be on the front lines of a battle. The defensive nature of her mech typically relegated her to the rear guard.

But this time, she had express permission from Touya, so it was fine to beat the enemies to a pulp.

"Touya's always been a little protective of me. I'm one of his fiancees, too! I'm plenty capable! A couple Upper Constructs aren't a problem for me!"

"Be careful... Don't get ahead of yourself... The Grand Duke worries about your rash nature..."

"Buh... I-I was just amping myself up! I'm not getting ahead of myself!"

"Good..." Sakura's soft voice fed through the cockpit speaker, making Sue panic a little.

She did regret that she'd made such a childish comment. Sue was the youngest of Touya's fiancees, after all. Yumina and Lu were the next youngest, and they were two years older than her.

Even though there were only two years between them, Sue thought there was a vast gulf of maturity between her and them. She wasn't necessarily right about this, though. It was just how she saw it. Still, feelings like that made Sue impatient to grow up faster. She wanted to become more ladylike, just like the girls older than her.

She'd recently asked her mother Ellen to teach her sewing, proper dancing form, and proper etiquette. The results weren't exactly befitting a noble lady, though...

"Well, whatever! Time to crush that beetle!"

Sue rapidly operated the command console within her customized cockpit. She poured magic through her fingers as she inputted various commands.

"Cannon Knuckle Spiral!"

Ortlinde Overlord's right arm began spinning rapidly before launching off at the elbow. The shining golden right hook flew into the stag beetle, smashing against the surface of its body.

The right hand whirred against the beetle's carapace for two full seconds before pulling back, failing to penetrate it. The enemy's body had cracks all over it, but they regenerated in no time at all. It eventually returned to an unhurt appearance.

"Hrm. Guess it can't be beaten that easily."

With regular Phrase, destroying the core was enough to kill them. It was the same with the mutants, but since they weren't see-through, it was hard to track their weak spots.

Plus, the Upper Constructs usually had multiple cores, so they were even trickier to deal with.

At a glance, it was easy to assume they wouldn't be in the legs or mandibles. They'd probably be in the torso or abdomen.

"If only I could locate the cores."

"I can handle that... Rossweisse is a support Frame Gear, so it can do that kind of thing..."

"It can, Sakura?"

More musical magic came from Sakura's Frame Gear.

The song was the main theme of a movie about a guy who went to the past in a car-shaped time machine. It spread out across the battlefield in a vibrant way, befitting the title "The Power of Love." Then, it washed over the Upper Construct.

It wasn't an offensive ability, so it simply ran through the beetle's body like a light, pinpointing the location of its cores.

"There are three cores... One in the head... and two in the chest... They're positioned in a vertical line, spaced out a bit... I'll send the readings."

"Neat."

One of Sue's monitors displayed an image of the Upper Construct. Three glowing dots were highlighted on the image, showing the core locations.

"Now I can aim and hit them properly. Just need to figure out a proper attack."

Sue grumbled a bit at her screen. It took considerable power to smash through an Upper Construct mutant and reach the cores inside.

Even with Sakura's music strengthening Ortlinde, she wasn't sure if she could do it alone. Plus, all three cores needed to be shattered one after the other, and fast. Otherwise, the regeneration would just kick in.

She was thinking maybe she should move the drill bits from Mjolnir, the subterranean tank that made up Ortlinde's legs, to Ortlinde's arm. Then, she could use a cannon knuckle spiral...

"I had a feeling it might end up like this!"

"Huh?! Wh-Wh-What?!"

Sue was startled by the sudden voice from the speakers. The voice belonged to High Rosetta, the lead maintainer of the Frame Gears and manager of the workshop.

"We made a special tool for the Ortlinde Overlord, yessir we did! Time to hammer that button! Whammo!"

Babylon, which floated high in the sky above the battlefield, fired a weapon down to the ground. It landed right in front of Ortlinde Overlord, kicking up sand everywhere.

The sound it made at first was a gigantic thud. Then, as the rest of it fell, it was more of a metallic clinking.

"That's…"

The weapon was a gigantic metal ball with a golden luster. It was attached to a giant chain. The weapon could be called a morning star, but it was positively enormous. It was truly a weapon befitting the Ortlinde Overlord.

"Yessir, we really went and did it! It's the anti-Upper Construct giga gravity weapon, the gold hammer!"

If Sue had more knowledge, she might have responded with "That's more of a throwing hammer than an actual hammer!"

"The gold hammer uses [Gravity] and [Prison] to accumulate magi-graviton energy in its ball component as it swings around. Then, when it hits its target, it'll unleash all the accumulated energy and crush the target to dust, yessir it will! The more you spin it, the stronger it'll get… But if you swing it too much, Ortlinde Overlord won't be able to heft it anymore. You gotta be careful, yessir you do!"

Sue didn't fully understand Rosetta's explanation, but she understood that she had a powerful weapon at her disposal.

Ortlinde Overlord picked up the chain handle of the gold hammer. The chain's length reached up to the Frame Gear's chest. The ball lifted with relative ease, so it seemed to be a reasonable weight for the time being.

Even in that state, it would be a devastating weapon to any regular enemy, but an Upper Construct would need further strength.

"Alright! Time to be a brave and noble lady… Let's go!"

The Ortlinde Overlord began to spin the gold hammer around. It started by swinging the weapon back and forth like a pendulum to pick up momentum.

Slowly, the gold circle began to spin around in a full circle, picking up speed and kicking up sand in the wake of its wind current.

The hammer's position shifted to a horizontal rotation without losing any momentum. Sparks began flying from the golden ball, and Ortlinde's arm started accumulating severe mechanical strain.

Sue could tell immediately that the weapon was building up massive force inside. The [**Prison**] enchantment was keeping that energy stored inside.

The stag beetle started generating light inside its mandibles. Much like the Dragon earlier, it was trying to unleash a particle beam laser.

"Oh no you dooon't!"

Ortlinde Overlord began to shift, spinning its entire body around like a spinning top to add more force to the gold hammer. And, after reaching the maximum limit that Ortlinde could take, the weapon was let go, flying toward the stag beetle along with all its magi-graviton mass.

The gold hammer struck true, flying like a bullet into the Upper Construct. Dark particles flowed from the gold hammer on impact, the sheer force of it distorting reality itself around the mutant foe.

A furious shockwave shook the very space in the surrounding area.

The body of the stag beetle began to crumble into fine grains before blowing away like dust in the wind. Every part of the creature, cores included, had been turned into powder.

"Crumble to dust!"

The twisted, distorted region of space destroyed the stag beetle instantly. When it finally subsided, there was nothing left but the gentle whoosh of nearby waves.

It was complete and utter obliteration. Despite Sue's words, there wasn't even dust left. It was simply gone.

The gold hammer itself ended up disintegrating as well. It seemed even the weapon couldn't withstand the force of the energy it was designed to contain.

"I did it, Touya! I did it! Wait, huh?"

Sue started celebrating in the cockpit, but Ortlinde Overlord suddenly fell to its knees. Steam and mana particles began rising from its joints, and the armor on its limbs began crumbling away.

All the monitors and displays inside the cockpit turned off, and the entire machine switched to emergency power.

"Huh? Why's it not moving?!"

"No need to worry about it, ma'am! That's just the recoil from using the gold hammer, yessir it is! Ortlinde's just overheated for a bit, that's all! Seems like we'll have to tweak Ortlinde a bit more so it can handle the collapsing energy!"

Sue opened up the cockpit hatch and hopped out of the immobile Frame Gear. The battle was still going on over at the main beach, so she could see the figures of Chevaliers taking on Lesser Construct mutants.

"Good work…"

A light pink Frame Gear appeared below Sue. It was Sakura's Rossweisse.

Sue pouted a little as she leaned against Ortlinde's chest hatch.

"I'm glad I beat that beetle, but I can't help Touya and the others now!"

"Don't worry… I'll go help them on your behalf…"

"No fair!"

Sue knew it was childish, but she couldn't help but throw a little tantrum. After all, she'd been waiting a while to make an impact with the others.

"It's okay... You did good, Sue. Be proud... Monica, please send Ortlinde Overlord and its pilot back to the hangar..."

"Roger!"

"Hey... Wait, I'm not done sulking!"

The kneeling titan, along with Sue, was wrapped up in glimmering light and warped away from the beach.

Sakura's Rossweisse was left behind, ready to continue supporting her allies.

"Now then... Should I help Elze's group or go to the Grand Duke...? Or wait, maybe I should support Yumina and the knights...?"

Sakura used search magic within the Rossweisse cockpit to get a grasp on the situation.

There was no reason to worry about Elze's group. Elze, Hilde, and Yae were an unstoppable trio when it came to physical combat.

However, Sakura was even less worried about Touya. There was no way he would ever lose a fight. Hell would surely freeze over before that happened. Sakura's belief in her fiance teetered on the verge of unwavering, blind faith.

With all that in mind, it was most logical for her to follow up with Yumina and the knight orders. Rossweisse specialized in support from the back, so she'd be able to make best use of her Frame Gear in a large-scale battle like that.

Sakura quietly affirmed that course of action before rushing back toward the carnage.

"It really is massive, it is…" When she saw it from Schwertleite's cockpit monitor, Yae couldn't stop herself from commenting on the starfish-shaped Upper Construct.

It resembled a pentagram from above, but from the sides it looked almost like a small mountain.

It slowly rotated its body as it floated slightly above the beach, sending sand everywhere. Its muddy-gold body shimmered in the sunlight.

"How will we handle this?"

"No point wasting time wondering about it! We gotta hit before we get hit, let's go! [**Boost**]!" Elze's crimson Frame Gear, Gerhilde, charged toward the starfish with the vernier thruster on its back. She moved as swiftly as ever.

"[**Fighting Spirit**]! Take this, [**Cannon Break**]!" Gerhilde's right fist enveloped itself in chi, smashing into one of the starfish's limbs.

The pile bunker on Gerhilde's right arm flew forward and smashed further into the Upper Construct's body. Cracks started spreading out across its surface.

"And here's another!" Gerhilde dug its feet into the sand before following up with a strike from its left fist. The pile bunker on the left arm echoed the movement of its right-arm counterpart, driving deeper cracks through the enemy's form.

Muddy-gold fragments splintered to the ground, and the tip of the starfish's arm fell off entirely.

"Guh…" Unfortunately, the limb regenerated even as the broken parts melted into sludge below.

"Figured I wouldn't get lucky and find a core there, huh." Elze jumped Gerhilde back, grumbling softly.

"It's okay, sis! The regeneration you just caused helped me trace the cores!" Linze spoke through the comms from above. She'd been using Helmwige to observe the enemy from above.

Regular and mutant Phrase alike needed to divert magical power from their cores to regenerate. That meant tracing the flow of magic through their bodies would allow you to find where their cores were.

"It seems like there's one in the middle, and one in each of its five legs." There were six cores in total. That was a lot, even for an Upper Construct.

"Six, huh? And we must destroy all of them at once, yes?" Hilde muttered to herself from inside Siegrune's cockpit.

"Linze, do you think we can call over Leen and use the Brionac?" Brionac was an enormous magical cannon. It was a guaranteed one-shot weapon that made use of the [Spiral] and [Explosion] spells to fire a specially-charged drillbit bullet.

It could only be used by Leen and Linze at the same time, since it required massive amounts of magical energy to activate. Even then it only allowed for one shot, making it pretty unwieldy in general.

"We could do that, but… We only have one shot, and if we leave behind even one core then it would've been wasted…"

"Hm… The battle would definitely be harder if Leen-dono and Linze-dono were put out of action, it would…"

"Everyone, look out!" Hilde suddenly yelled out, prompting the others to look at the starfish. It had stopped rotating.

Its five limbs started cracking before splitting from the middle and falling to the ground at the tips. Each limb-tip was loosely connected to the middle portion by stringy, muddy-gold tentacles.

Those tips reared upward like snake heads.

Suddenly particles of light began gathering at the end of each.

163

"Ah?! We must dodge, we must!" Yae yelled out, and everyone in the area scattered.

The tips of the disconnected limbs fired out thin lasers, weaker than the ones from the Dragon.

Everyone in the vicinity could hear a sickening hissing sound as the very sand around them melted into goopy puddles.

"Watch out! Incoming!" Elze cried out.

The limb-tips swiveled around and started charging up laser blasts once again.

Five lasers began cutting through the air, headed directly for Yae and the other Valkyrie gears.

"Lestian Sacred Sword: Second Wardance!" Hilde leaped from the beach in her Siegrune, slicing one of the tentacles and bringing the detached limb-tip crashing to the ground.

The tip was then slashed into ribbons in the blink of an eye, melting down into goop on the beach. A small red orb, two meters in diameter, was among the goo. It melted down too.

But the smashed limb-tip quickly regenerated, returning to its former appearance in seconds. The core was regenerated inside it as well, so they were back to square one.

The whole group jumped back to put some distance between them and the lasers.

"Just as we'd thought... Destroying one limb does nothing."

"Yeah, we're gonna have to get them all at once."

"But there's only four of us."

"Then we need two more, we do... Shall we ask Yumina-dono, Lu-dono, or Leen-dono for aid?" With two more, or even with one more, they could launch a coordinated attack on all five limbs at once. Then they'd be able to quickly go for the central core as a group before it regenerated itself.

But given the current battle situation, it'd be hard for Yumina, Leen, and Lu to leave their support roles with the knights.

"Two more, huh? How about us?"

All the girls cried out in sudden, surprised unison.

They had no idea where the source of that voice had come from.

As if out of nowhere, there was someone standing on Schwertleite's shoulder. There was someone standing on Siegrune's shoulder too.

One held a three-meter crystal blade, certainly not something you'd expect a woman of her build to be carrying. The other held a large bow in her hands, and a mighty quiver on her back.

"Moroha-aneue and Karina-dono?! How long have you been here, how long?" Yae stared in wide-eyed shock at the sight of her fiance's elder sister atop her Frame Gear.

"We weren't planning to help at first, but sitting around and watching just wasn't enough... I came by hoping to mop up a couple weaklings or something."

"Moroha called me over. It'll be a nice way to while away some time, though." The two of them spoke playfully, since it was basically just fun sport to them. They were both strong enough to claim something like that fairly easily.

"So if the five of us go for the limbs, then Karina can shoot an arrow for the middle, so..."

"No can do! We're just here to support you, so we're not gonna do anything that extreme. The one to land the final hit, let's see... Linze. You can do it."

"What...?! M-M-Me?!" Linze practically shrieked in response. Karina spoke so casually about it, but Linze fully knew that if she screwed up the last hit, then they'd be back at square one again.

That was quite the burden for a timid girl like her.

"Just be calm and it'll work out. You've been through some hard times, right? But you made it through. I think you'll be okay. Why don't you show Touya how much you've grown?"

"O-Okay!" Linze answered with renewed vigor.

"Alrighty then. Then me, Elze, Hilde, Karina, and Yae will go for the cores in its limbs. When we do that, Linze'll go for the center core. Got it?" Moroha grinned as she spoke, hefting her sword over her shoulder. Hilde was a little confused as to how they were hearing Moroha so clearly when she wasn't using a communicator, but she chalked it up to divinity stuff and didn't think too hard about it.

Moroha and Karina leaped down to the ground.

Karina pulled out two bevel nata blades from nowhere, and wielded them in each hand.

She deftly deflected several lasers using her newly-manifested crystal weapons.

The four fiancees stared at Karina from inside their cockpits, dumbfounded by her incredible skill. They eventually chalked it up to divinity stuff and didn't think too hard about it.

"Alright. Let's hustle. Everyone except Linze, spread out and destroy your target core within a minute. Got that?!"

"Gotcha!"

"Very well!"

"I understand, I do!"

"We got this!"

"Y-Yes, we'll be fine!"

"Then let's go, ladies!" Two goddesses, and three Frame Gears, charged along the sandy beach.

The starfish's limbs darted after them, hunting them down with laser strikes. But each and every one of the girls managed to dodge, deflect, or slice back. There was actually only one of them who managed to cut the laser, though. But that wasn't really a big deal.

"Kokonoe Secret Style: Sword Flash!" The first one to make her way through was Yae in her Schwertleite. She tore through one of the muddy-gold appendages with strikes swifter than the naked eye.

Yae immediately spotted the exposed core, and stabbed her katana right through it.

The core raised a loud shattering noise and crumbled into pieces. That was one down.

"[Boost]!" Next came Elze in Gerhilde. She pummeled the limb firing lasers at her with the pile bunkers.

She started with punches clad in divinity, and drove her pile bunkers into the cracks. It could hardly even be called a fight; it was almost like deep excavation or mining work. She was pulling chunk after chunk of corrupted phrasium from her enemy's body.

"There it is!" The core became dislodged and rolled out of the limb. Gerhilde scooped her right arm upward and struck the core with her uppercut. Two down.

"Hup, hup..." Karina ran across the sand on foot, deflecting laser after laser as they fired her way. She displayed every instinct one might expect from a hunting goddess, tracking her prey with merciless precision.

Karina jumped into the air, landing atop the wriggling limb. She brought her machete down, splitting it like chopped firewood. The core within was sliced down the middle. It crumbled instantly. It was a casual and anticlimactic finish. Just another successful hunt. Three down.

"Lestian Sacred Sword: Fifth Swirl!" Hilde charged forward in her orange Siegrune, clashing head-on against her target.

It brandished a crystal blade in its hand, creating a spinning wind around it and splitting apart the muddied phrasium.

The red core was swept by the updraft, casting it into the sky above.

"Hmph!" Siegrune's blade danced through the air, cleanly splitting the core in half as it fell back to earth. Four down.

"Good job, girls. Now I'll go for mine…" Moroha smiled broadly, casually swinging her forty-centimeter-wide blade and slicing apart the lasers that came toward her.

Once again, very casually, she swung her blade in the direction of her target. Even though there was still a considerable distance between them, the shockwave from her motion sliced the limb to pieces.

Her attack, which seemed to rend space itself, cleanly split the core in half. Five down.

Moroha, who hadn't moved a single step throughout all of that, looked up to Helmwige.

"Looks like it's time for the finale." Linze knew from Helmwige's readings that the central core had begun sending out magical pulses to regenerate the rest of the body. The final core was smack-bang in the middle, she needed to hurry.

If the regeneration was allowed to continue, then everyone else's hard work would have all been for nothing. She couldn't afford to lose here.

"… H-Here I go!" Linze gripped the controls in front of her and started a sudden descent toward the starfish.

She focused all her attention on the monitor, lining up the sights for her revolver cannons.

The moment the sights lined up with the core's location, Linze pulled the trigger and held it down for dear life.

Pew, pew, pew, pew!! The hail of crystal bullets fired in rapid succession, raining down upon their target.

The middle of the starfish's body was dented and pelted by bullet after bullet.

Eventually the muddy-gold shell gave way to the red core. But Helmwige's furious flurry of bullets didn't stop, landing blow after blow on to the exposed weak point and cracking it.

But the central core was roughly twice the size of the other cores. It wouldn't break as easily. If Linze didn't do something, the other cores would regenerate before she succeeded.

"I won't… Give you the chance!" Linze suddenly had Helmwige shift from flight mode into regular Frame Gear mode.

The shift in forms meant that Helmwige was no longer capable of flight, and it would come crashing down to the ground. But that was exactly what Linze wanted.

"Hiyaaaah!!" Linze cried out with righteous force, and expertly navigated a drop kick on to the cracked core below.

This technique was something Linze had learned without even realizing it. After all, she had been carefully watching her older sister's training more than anyone else. It was the ultimate crystallization of her bond with Elze. An attack picked up simply by paying close attention to her sister's style.

The incredible hit utterly obliterated the central core. With that, the starfish-shaped Upper Construct was done for.

The great creature's body began melting down into sludge. All the participants in its death moved away and watched it from afar.

"You did it, Linze! That was totally awesome!"

"You truly resembled Elze-dono, you did. What a wonderful attack."

"Indeed. It was quite the amazing strike. I knew you could do it."

"R-Really? Ahaha… I got so into it, it was like my body moved on its own. I'm really happy it worked out…" Linze blushed a little, but she was smiling.

Thus, they had won their fight. Linze turned her gaze toward the shoreline, and she saw that Touya's fight against the two-headed Dragon was drawing to a close as well.

The two-headed Dragon launched bladed spines toward Reginleif.

But the twelve crystal spheres orbiting the Frame Gear easily countered them.

The Fragarachs had taken sphere form, and operated as autonomous defensive satellites.

"Alrighty. Time to wrap this up… I need to check in on Ende, and I'm a bit worried about the knights too." The battle was shifting to our favor. Unfortunately, the Lesser and Intermediate Constructs had been stronger than we'd anticipated. Some of our knights had been overpowered, but things still looked positive.

Sue and Elze's teams had wrapped up their battles, so they'd definitely be able to go help the regular knights. I needed to hurry up and go help the others.

The two-headed Dragon opened both of its mouths, preparing for another beam blast.

"Nope, not happening." The twelve spheres transformed into two lances that propelled themselves toward the gaping mouths.

The lances crashed their way into the Dragon's maws before spreading open like umbrellas and starting to rotate.

The two lances began drilling through muddy-gold carapace until they pierced through the backs of the Dragon's throats.

Both heads cracked and shattered above the jaw, and they melted into sludge like usual.

But the broken pieces immediately regenerated and reformed the heads in no time at all. I wasn't exactly surprised, but it was worth a shot.

"Now, let's see about those cores…"

I used my divine sight to look the Dragon up and down. Chest, belly, and tail… There were three in total. It was a little annoying, but easily manageable.

I called one of the two lances to Reginleif's hand, and transformed the other into twenty-four daggers.

I then merged those daggers with the lance, and formed a much larger heavy lance.

"Alright, let's do this." I charged toward the two-headed Dragon, heavy lance in hand.

I smashed Reginleif right into the Dragon's chest, caving it in slightly through sheer force of momentum.

It had a tough exterior, but I'd expected that. The defense was certainly higher around its chest than it was on its heads; even the heavy lance wasn't working its way through the damn thing's body as fast as I wanted. I wished it would just die faster so I could get to the others.

"Apotheosis!" Reginleif suddenly found itself surrounded by my divinity. With that, the heavy lance started to cut through my enemy's body like butter.

The lance kept sliding through the corrupted phrasium until its tip pressed against the chest core.

"Shatter!" Reginleif mercilessly shattered the core to bits.

I quickly turned the lance around with a swift U-turn, and then I charged back toward the Dragon.

This time I was aiming for the core in its belly.

The heavy lance used its divinity-clad aura to shatter the carapace and meet its mark.

Reginleif pushed onward, smashing through the other side of the Dragon, crushing the second core in the process.

"It's over for you now." Reginleif turned once more, and flew toward the Dragon's tail like an arrow.

The tail core was much less protected than the other two, and thus it took only a simple thrust from the heavy lance to obliterate it.

Black smoke began rising up from the two-headed Dragon as it crumbled.

The last of the Upper Constructs had fallen, bubbling down into waxy goop.

"That was pretty easy, huh. Now then… Time to go help every-"

"Touya! Three-o'clock! One of the mutants!" Yumina alerted me to an Intermediate Construct shaped like a sea anemone. It had two Chevaliers caught in its tentacle-like snares.

The tentacles sucked both Frame Gears into the mutant's body, absorbing them in a matter of seconds.

"Flora! Are those pilots okay?!" Flora was stationed at the emergency medical center on the beach.

"They're okay, you see. The two of them used their emergency escape devices." I was relieved to hear that. Deaths may have been an inevitability when it came to some wars, but I still wanted to keep any losses to a minimum.

The Frame Gears that got eaten were from Brunhild. It had probably taken advantage of an opening in their defenses when the two of them were moving to support others.

The tentacled anemone looked a little tougher than the rest of them.

I hefted the heavy lance and prepared to take it out, but it suddenly started moving strangely.

It began backing away from the shoreline and heading into the sea.

I watched it, confused, as something worse suddenly happened. Space itself cracked around the anemone, creating a rift in the air.

The sea anemone shuffled backward into the space between worlds, vanishing into the crack with the two Chevaliers it had stolen.

And then, like a video being rewound, the crack in space sealed itself back up again. The anemone had escaped.

"Wait, was that…?"

I was frozen in shock by the unexpected event. I'd seen something behind the anemone, through the gap in space. It was distinctly humanoid. It was probably another Dominant Construct, lurking in the shadows. "…Worrying about it won't do anything. We need to get this battle finished." I tuned Reginleif's communicator to the general channel.

"The Upper Constructs are all dead! This isn't a battle anymore, it's a hunt! Wipe out all the remaining enemies, don't leave any alive!"

"HOO-RAH!" The knights all roared ferociously. The Frame Gears all charged ahead with renewed vigor, smashing mutant after mutant.

We'd already dealt with around eighty percent of them. The only major part of this conflict was in the hands of Ende and his group.

I shifted my Fragarachs to daggers and sent them to support the knights. As I maneuvered the blades, I activated my divine sight to look over to the [Prison] Ende was battling inside.

It was a little rude to peek on them, but I was a bit concerned.

The [**Prison**] was cut off from the outside world, but my divine sight allowed me to view the unusual battle going on within.

"Leto. Luto. It's been some time." Melle raised her voice, but the twin Dominants only replied with smirks.

"Before I left Phrasia, did I not entrust you two with the duty of advising the new Sovereign? What happened?"

"Haaaah. Do you really think that we wanted to babysit your successor? We wanted something more fun, something more engaging."

"Indeed. That's why we joined Yula in crossing worlds. Yula, Gila, and even Ney so earnestly went out there to search for you... But we didn't care about that at all. We saw a golden opportunity, you see. We realized that we didn't have to exercise restraint in these new worlds we'd cross through."

Melle narrowed her eyes in response.

"And just where is Yula now, hm? Isn't he the one behind all of this?"

"Who knows? We don't exactly interact with him very often. Ever since Yula gained this golden power, he's been off doing all kinds of things. We don't know the details, and we don't care," Melle said, then sighed quietly. She knew that Yula had always been a secretive sort. But she was a little surprised that he hadn't revealed any of his plans to the twins, who were supposed to be his allies.

Back on Phrasia, Yula was considered the most accomplished scientist around. Even Melle couldn't help but be impressed by his endless thirst for knowledge.

But that thirst paved the way for a dark obsession. Yula would sacrifice anything, employ any method, all without regret. If it was for the sake of discovery, he'd use and abuse anything he could get his hands on. His heart was clearly ice cold.

"It doesn't really matter to us what Yula is doing. Isn't that right, brother dearest? So long as we're having fun, we don't really have any complaints. Now then, is that all you wanted to ask us? Can we get around to killing you now? In truth, we don't really need the Sovereign's power anymore, but it might be a nice little addition to our forces if we can claim your core here and now."

"If you so much as touch Lady Melle, I'll take your cores and crush them into dust."

"My, you certainly do talk the talk. Pity you can't walk the walk, Ney." Leto taunted Ney with a smug, sadistic grin.

Ney glared back with fury boiling over behind her eyes.

Luto, who stood by his sister, suddenly turned his gaze toward Ende.

"We allowed you to escape last time, Endymion. But this time we'll ensure you meet your end. It might be a little nice if we gut you in front of the Sovereign, don't you think? It would add a little spice to the confrontation. But, hm… How shall we kill you? There are so many methods to pick from."

"Yeah, I gotta admit I'm stuck thinking too, you mutated bastard. I'm wondering just how I should go about beating the crystal snot out of you." Ende rolled his shoulders and spoke casually, refusing to give in to Luto's provocation.

Luto adopted a slightly frustrated expression, staring Ende down and spitting a few words back.

"Did we give you brain damage or something? How exactly do you intend to hurt us, hm? You couldn't do a thing last time."

"Well, I was thinking I'd get right up close to you like this." Ende suddenly appeared in front of Luto; it was as if he hadn't moved his body at all. His motion was so swift it resembled teleportation.

"Wha-?!"

"And then I was thinking of putting all my power behind a right hook." Before Luto could even react, Ende's arm had pulled back and pushed forward, slamming a clenched fist right into the Dominant Construct's cheek.

Luto flew backward, his neck bent at an odd angle. He writhed slightly as he rolled along the ground.

"Brother dearest?!" Luto kept crashing and rolling along the ground until he hit the wall of the [Prison] and finally stopped. Leto looked on in shock.

He scrambled to his feet and glared in confusion over toward Ende. Deep cracks ran through the carapace on his right cheek, but they quickly mended themselves.

"You wretch… How dare you?!"

"Don't get mad because you can't walk the walk, Luto. Anger clouds one's judgment, you know. Emotional weakness creates physical weakness in the heat of combat. That's one of the things my master taught me."

"Don't talk down to me! Don't get so conceited, you little shit!" Luto snarled, kicking up off the ground and madly charging at Ende. He swung out his right fist toward Ende's face, almost in an attempt to pay him back for the earlier blow.

But, just at the last second before impact, Ende caught the incoming strike with his palm.

"Wh-?!"

"That's it? Elze is a lot scarier when she uses her [Boost] spell. If I couldn't block something as weak as that, then my master would definitely chew me out about it." Luto's eyes widened as his confusion deepened, and Ende was quick to take advantage of that. The white-haired youth spun around and delivered a brutal backspin kick to the Phrase's lower back.

"Bwugh!" Luto was blasted back yet again, kicking up sand as he rolled along the dunes.

"Guh!" His sister, Leto, attempted to rush to his aid. But she found her path blocked by Lycee and Ney.

"Out of my way! Move!" Leto suddenly reshaped her arm into a wretched-looking muddy-gold blade. She brought it swinging down toward Ney.

Even though it was only a trace amount, that blade was imbued with the wicked god's divinity. Ney was a Dominant Construct, but she was far less than the divine. If she didn't dodge, there's no way her body would be able to resist the slash.

But... What Leto felt in the next instant was not the satisfaction of having cleaved through her enemy. She felt a hard resistance against her limb, and a clashing sound.

She looked at her arm in confusion, and saw Ney blocking it with a sword.

Ney smiled wide, almost laughing at her mutated foe.

"I was a bit worried for a sec, but it looks like Touya was right! It worked!"

"J-Just what is that blade?!" Leto swung her sword-arm again, and then a third time. But the silver-white blade in Ney's hand parried the hit at every turn. That was to be expected, of course, for Ney's blade was no ordinary weapon.

It was one of the sacred treasure blades that Ende had pilfered from another world after his loss to the twins.

Touya had taken them back after all that business was dealt with, but he'd allowed Lycee and Ney to borrow them for this battle.

Even if they were Dominant Constructs, they were still Phrase lifeforms. That meant there was a chance they could be consumed by the mutants, or converted. Touya decided that granting them the divine weapons would give them the necessary protection. After all, the blades had just been laying around in his [Storage]. So Touya got permission from the other gods and had then handed them over.

"You know, Ney. I've been thinking about this for a while, but... You and your little friends really piss me and my brother off! You're always getting in the way of our fun!"

"That's really funny, actually. I was just thinking about how much you piss me off! How you always did whatever you wanted, and how you never gave Lady Melle the proper respect. We were allies before so I put up with it, but now you're my enemy... So I can tear you apart and finally be rid of you!"

"Shut the hell up, bitch!" Leto screeched, flailing her sword-arm furiously in Ney's direction.

Even though Ney had a sacred treasure, Leto was still a lot stronger than her. It was taking all of her power just to deflect the strikes raining down on her.

But, taking advantage of Leto's distracted state, Lycee took her chance to strike. She slashed at the blade-arm, severing it cleanly and saving Ney from further peril.

Leto's right arm thudded to the ground and began melting into slime.

"Gh... I didn't even notice you! You always have been forgettable, you bitch!" Leto jumped back, regrowing her missing arm in a flash.

Lycee stared back at her, brandishing the divine blade in her hands.

"Are you okay, Ney?"

"Yeah. I'm okay, somehow... Couldn't you have helped a little sooner?"

"You two were having a conversation, I didn't want to interrupt..."

"Th-That wasn't really a conversation..." Ney was a little bewildered by Lycee's nonsensical reasoning, but she just shrugged it off.

Even back on Phrasia, Lycee was considered an oddball.

She wasn't a bad girl by any means, but she often behaved in an atypical way. Hell, she'd even been part of Yula's group with Ney, but somehow she ended up joining Endymion without anyone noticing.

Ney originally believed she'd been tricked by Ende into doing that, but she couldn't exactly deny that Lycee probably did it on her own. Still, Ney would take any chance she could get to yell at or punch Ende, so she was happy to pretend like he was a bad influence on the girl.

"Hm? So you'll both be facing me? Very well. If you want to fight so bad, let's make it a real one!" Leto's body shifted as a muddy-gold metal spilled out from inside her. It began coating her, fixing jagged armored pieces onto her arms, legs, torso and more.

In a short while, every part of her body aside from her face had been covered in the thicker material. It was some kind of enhanced version of the crystal armor that other Dominants could equip.

"You bastard, Endymion! Don't you dare mess around with me! You're nothing, you hear me?! Nothing! Gahahahah!!" Ney and the others glanced over toward the sudden yelling, and saw Luto clashing with Ende. He'd covered himself in the golden armor as well. It certainly wasn't surprising that the two of them were so synchronized.

"Now, let's take this from the top. I'll crush you to bits, Endymion."

"Indeed, it's as my dear brother says. Lycee, Ney. I'll pulverize your cores. I'll eat you alive."

Luto VS Ende

Leto VS Ney and Lycee

The Sovereign stood away and watched. The battle within the [**Prison**] was about to reach fever pitch.

Luto charged ahead, morphing both of his arms into blades.

The Phrase's crystal armor was a technique that took the life energy from inside a Phrase's core, and projected it outwardly.

It was similar to the fighting spirit used by Elze and Ende.

Luto, having imbued himself with this armament chi, was now capable of phenomenal strength and explosive speed.

"Raaargh!" Luto slashed toward Ende. Unlike Ney and Lycee, Ende wasn't wielding any divine weapons. If he took a strike like that, then he'd surely be torn asunder.

However… Ende didn't move from his position. He simply exhaled deeply and focused all his power within a spot beneath his navel.

"Fighting Spirit: Energy Release!"

"What?!" Ende's body began to emanate chi as he garbed himself in raw fighting spirit. But this wasn't any ordinary chi; it had divinity mixed into it. It wasn't pure like Touya's, but it was more than enough to contend with the wicked god's muddied force. This martial chi was truly befitting of the god of combat's disciple.

Ende's hands, clad in fighting spirit, clapped down on the incoming blade and caught it. It was almost like a magic trick, but this was the real deal.

"Haaah!"

"Nh?!" Ende then twisted both of his hands, and broke off the arm-blade. He tossed the blade aside before smacking the back of his hand into Luto's face.

Luto's shattered arm started regenerating as he flew backward. He rolled on the ground a few times before steadying himself and standing.

Luto turned back toward Ende, but suddenly his body spasmed. An impact crater appeared on his right shoulder, as if an invisible fist had hammered into it.

"Guh! Wh-What is this?!"

"Dang, I missed. Seems like my energy release isn't quite good enough for combat yet." Ende grumbled quietly, his right arm extended. The further the distance, the lower the accuracy and strength. His abilities still weren't refined enough to use at range. It was easier for him to just directly punch his enemies.

"Now, let me pay you back for the time you two messed me up." Ende ran full pelt at Luto. Luto was powered up, though, so he could now read Ende's movements.

His newly-regenerated arm had been specially grown to be more dense and durable. He was prepared for the incoming strike.

Ende's punch connected with the defensive arm. It groaned and cracked slightly, but it didn't break.

He then took his chance to send a thorn-studded punch right back toward Ende.

But his white-haired foe dodged the strike just barely, spinning in place and turning Luto's world upside down.

"Gwuh?!" Luto slammed into the ground, finding himself the sudden and swift victim of an over-shoulder throw.

Ende tried to follow up with a downward punch against his fallen foe, but he had to jump back to avoid the laser blast coming his way from the side.

The terrible heat ray pierced the space that had previously been occupied by Ende's head.

The laser carried on until it hit the [**Prison**] wall and dissipated.

Ende turned toward the source of the blast, and he saw Leto staring at him incredulously.

"Die, vermin!" She began charging up another blast at the tip of her blade-arm.

Ende dodged it with a swift backstep, putting distance between him and Luto.

Luto then used that opportunity to scramble to his feet and slash his blade arm at Ney, who was in the middle of charging toward his sister.

"Guh!" Ney used her divine weapon to parry the blade arm. Luto quickly changed his strategy, reaching out his arm further to wrap around his sister's body. He pulled her toward him.

Leto flew upward, spun in midair, and landed next to her twin.

"Crud, I wanted to beat them while they were separated..." Ende grumbled a little as he looked over at the twins. They'd taken a defensive posture, standing back to back.

They were twins, and they seemed to have perfect teamwork. When they worked together, they could perform far more than twice as efficiently than they could alone.

"Sorry. We couldn't keep her held down."

"Yeah, sorry."

"It's alright. I couldn't take out Luto, either." Ende stood opposite Ney and Lycee; they surrounded the twins on either side.

Ende maintained his aura of fighting spirit, kicking off from the ground and charging forward. Luto came swiping at him with his sword arm, but Ende's divinity-laden fist tanked the attack with little difficulty.

Luto was rendered defenseless, leaving him open for Ende to kick his side.

But... Leto moved from behind her brother, and jabbed her sword arm toward Ende like a spear.

"Gah!" Ende had to contort his entire body just to avoid the strike. He retreated on the spot.

Leto had attacked Ende without even looking in Luto's direction. She kept her gaze trained on Ney and Lycee, but still managed to effortlessly intercept Ende's attack.

"These guys are a real pain…"

"I believe that should be our line. I'm angry that you meaningless little mooks have harmed us to this degree. Yula would laugh if he learned about this. Leto, sister dearest! It is time to put an end to this!"

"You're right, brother dearest. I'm getting quite tired of this. I'm especially irritated by that weak little woman just watching our battle from the sidelines. Let's play our final card."

Leto sneered directly toward Melle, who was hiding a good distance behind Lycee and Ney.

A cracking sound rang out as several crystal rods, around the size of bamboo reeds, started jutting out in a spiral pattern beneath the twins.

The rods pushed upward and upward, elevating the duo higher and higher, liquefying at the top and engulfing their bodies.

A single form remained after the grim transformation, revealing an eight-legged mass where the twins once stood.

It was a great spider. The twins' bodies from the waist upward jutted out above the spider abdomen and thorax.

There was a demonkin species known as the Arachne. It had the upper body of a woman, and the lower body of a spider. The giant spider in front of them certainly resembled an Arachne, but it had two upper bodies that covered both sexes, and it was made of metallicized, muddy-gold phrasium.

"What is that, your true form or something?"

"This is a power granted to us by Yula. We've kept it sealed until now because we find it unsightly, but that matters not now. We're going to slaughter you and consume your wasting corpses!" Luto's voice was the most prominent, but there were traces of Leto's voice undertoning it. The twins had become one, in the most complete sense of the word.

Ende could trace the magic flow through its body. Their cores had been inside their throats when they had human forms, but now both cores had moved toward the spider body's center, and they were acting as one.

Leto's right arm morphed, and so did Luto's left. Before long, each arm took the form of a giant pair of scissors, two pairs in total.

They weren't animalistic pincers like a crab claw; they had straight-up become long, metallic scissors that you might find in a kitchen.

"Take this!" The closed pair of scissors jabbed toward Ende.

Ende leaped backward, causing the weapon to dig itself into the sand.

"We'll tear you in half!" Leto's voice was the more prominent sound in that scream, with a little bit of Luto's undertoning it.

The second pair of scissors came rushing forward, opening up wide and stretching toward Lycee.

"Lycee!" Ney ran toward her sister, who hadn't reacted well enough in time.

Leto's scissors weren't trying to cut Lycee down the middle; they were aiming for her neck. She was trying to instantly kill Lycee by shattering her core.

Even a Dominant Construct couldn't regenerate if their core was destroyed. The act would mean certain death.

Just as the scissors closed around Lycee's exposed throat, they stopped. A high-pitched sound rang out. It wasn't that they stopped of their own volition, it was more that they'd been stopped.

"Wh-?!" A phrasium pillar had emerged from the ground in front of Lycee, blocking Leto's scissor attack by catching the blades.

"Damn it!" Leto channeled more corrupted divinity into the blades, strengthening them. The pillar was destroyed. Fortunately, Lycee managed to escape within that time frame.

"You dare get in our way?!" Leto turned and glared toward the source of the phrasium pillar. It was Melle, the Phrase Sovereign.

"This was a battle that Endymion and the others wished to partake in. I intended to simply watch over it from afar... Or that was my excuse, anyway. But I think I need to re-evaluate my approach here. You two are still fellow Phrase, no matter your opinions. I suppose I've been unable to get over that hurdle, and I'm unable to bring myself to bear arms against you as a result."

"Pah. We've long since discarded the droll life of a mere phrasium lifeform. We have the power to do whatever we like."

"That's right! We're no longer shackled by that inferior life! We're finally free! We can kill all those that wrong us, rampage in lands yet unknown, live however we like! Most importantly, we need never serve a Sovereign like you ever again!"

"My... You two really are too far gone now, aren't you?" Melle sighed softly, looking down at the ground. She slowly raised her head and faced the beast before her.

"I am the Sovereign of all Phrase. Thus I must see to my duty and put an end to your carnage. Prisma Chain." Phrasium pillars began jutting out of the ground all over the place. The pillars transformed into connecting chain links that stretched out and attached to one another. They then shrank down, immobilizing the massive spider.

"Guh! You little bitch…!" The monstrous spider began to tear at the crystal chains binding it. Leto and Luto became so preoccupied with freeing themselves, that they didn't notice the white-haired young man with the trailing scarf charging toward them.

"Wh-?!"

"Sacred Combat Art… Divine Palm Spiral!" Ende held his palm up, gathering divinity inside it. The young man took a firm step forward and drove the swirling golden light into the spider's body.

A large impact rang out, but… Nothing seemed to happen. Leto and Luto were seemingly unharmed.

"And with that… I have my vengeance."

"What are you talking ab… Ugh?!"

"What? No… What have you done to us? This can't be, it isn't happening! No! We…" Leto and Luto began melting into thick, muddy goop.

The two of them realized what had happened in their last moments. Ende's palm strike had shattered their cores. No damage had been done to any other part of their body. The shockwave of divinity that had been pressed into them specifically targeted the points that would kill them.

The divinity of the wicked god, which had been protecting their cores, paled in comparison to the real divinity that Ende benefited from.

The spider body collapsed completely, black smoke hissing upward from it. Leto and Luto's original bodies lay there amidst the sludge, and soon they began to melt down themselves. They were unable to retain their own structural integrity.

They gasped and moaned, opening their mouths one final time in unison as if to say something… But no words ever came.

Ney looked away in sorrow and shame. Even though they'd pledged their souls to the wicked god, they were still her former allies. She quietly thought about how close she had been to meeting a similar fate.

When Ney finally opened her eyes, she just saw the soot-like outlines where their bodies once were. The twins, once Dominant Constructs just like her, had been snuffed out completely.

"Ney... You good?"

"...Yeah. I'm good." Ney gave Lycee a curt response. Even if they had a complicated relationship, Ney had known Luto and Leto for thousands of years. It was understandable she'd have mixed feelings about their deaths.

The bitter mood was suddenly broken by the appearance of a Frame Gear. It was Touya in his Reginleif.

"Looks like you guys are just about done."

"Yup. Same with you." Ende extended a thumbs-up in response to Touya's voice.

Just like that, the four walls of the [Prison] around them shimmered away like snow.

"We just need to mop up the stragglers now. You mind deploying your Dragoon to help?"

"Man, you can't let a guy rest at all, Touya. Yeah, I'll help. Just be sure to pay me for my services."

"Sure, sure. I'll treat you guys to whatever. Pork cutlets, tempura, grilled eel, you name it."

"...Why are you just listing off food? I mean, I understand why, but still..."

Ende sighed and glanced back at the three girls behind him. Even though they didn't take in any energy from calories, they still ate a lot of food. An overwhelming amount of the money

Ende earned from the adventurer's guild ended up going down their hungry gullets.

Ende had no doubt that the three of them could wolf down a whole Dragon without issue.

In the end, Ende shrugged his shoulders. He'd have preferred money, but it would probably end up getting spent on food anyway... Having Touya pay him with meals would save time for all parties involved.

"Guess that's the end of that." I leaned back in Reginleif's cockpit, summoning a map of the area on the central console. There wasn't a single enemy mutant left. We'd finished cleaning them up.

We'd suffered some damage, but nobody had died. The biggest losses were the two Chevaliers taken by that weird anemone, and the Ortlinde Overlord being pretty heavily damaged. A few of our other Chevaliers were considerably damaged too.

My head started to hurt just thinking about what would come next. First up we'd have to arrange a world leader summit to discuss our plans. I had a feeling that the leaders of the western continent would better understand the severity of the situation now, at least.

Given that two Frame Gears had been stolen, I wouldn't be surprised if we had Frame Gear-shaped mutants showing up at some point.

So now I had to think about a countermeasure for something like that... I just had to hope that Doctor Babylon would take care of it.

If Ende and the others were right, then the only Dominant Construct left was Yula, but something was bothering me...

The humanoid shape I saw when the anemone fled... It didn't feel like Yula at all.

It was possible he had called more Dominants from Phrasia to help him, but I didn't know what to make of the situation.

It was pointless worrying about it, though. We needed to act on what we did know, not ponder on what we didn't.

I flipped on the common channel along Reginleif's radio transmitter and spoke up.

"Attention all soldiers, our mission is complete. I'll trigger my magic to teleport you all back where you need to be, so hang tight."

It had been two days since we'd repelled the invasion. Several world leaders had gathered in Brunhild to discuss our plans.

As I'd expected, actually seeing such a terrible battle happen before their eyes was enough for the leaders of the western continent to understand the gravity of the threat. They were well aware that, unless we cooperate, the world could face ruin.

Primula, Triharan, Strain, Allent, Gardio, Lassei, and Panaches were all granted Frame Unit VR simulators to train their knights. I asked that they prepare squads to help fight in coming conflicts.

On the political side, things were all progressing smoothly... But not everything was going so well.

"Frame Gear mutants, hm... They may take that approach. After all, appropriating weaponry is a common tactic in warfare. Isn't this why I told you that our general infantry should have self-destruct buttons installed by default?!"

"I still think that's going too far..." I had a feeling that nobody would want to pilot our Frame Gears if they were rigged to blow.

I sighed quietly as Doctor Babylon mulled over blueprints on her desk.

"So… that Yula person, is he some kind of engineer?"

"Ah, well… According to Melle, he's like an engineer, a biologist, a politician, a smooth-talker… All kinds of stuff… A genius, essentially. Though apparently, Melle has always been more knowledgeable than him when it comes to more esoteric stuff like magic."

"Hrmph… And now that genius has a hold of my precious little Frame Gears, huh? He probably wants to tinker and change them. There sure are a lot of jerks out there who mooch off the hard work and technology of others and try to pass it off as their own? Isn't that right, Touya?"

Please don't guilt me like that… I know I've been re-inventing common Earth stuff over here, but gimme a break…

"Do you think he might be dabbling in Gollem technology as well?"

"Given the Isengard situation, it's likely."

"It's possible that he got interested in Frame Gears because he started looking at Gollems. Still, I have my pride as an engineer, you know?! I won't lose. That's why I need you to show me more visual references for my upcoming projects, okay?"

"Ugh…"

I grumbled quietly as Doctor Babylon inched closer and closer, steam practically firing out of her nose. It sure sounded proper when she said she wanted visual references, but she was basically just asking to watch more mecha anime.

I didn't mind showing them some more, but I didn't want them getting inspired by something weird. I mean, it was true that weird ideas had done pretty well for us in the past, but still…

I didn't want us to lose just because I'd been hesitant to help, so I begrudgingly agreed, leading all of them to the garden.

The usual suspects like Rosetta, Monica, and Elluka (with Fenrir) were gathered there. But I was surprised to find that Sue, Sakura, Linze, and Cesca were there as well. Even Paula and the heavenly beasts had tagged along.

"We're fans of this annie may stuff, too!" Linze spoke so excitedly that I dared not correct her. Now all I had to do was decide what to show them.

Cesca started preparing tea and snacks, so I started flicking my finger along my smartphone.

…This one won't do. I don't wanna show something scary like a planet getting cleaved in half. Plus, the ending to this one is so sad that Sue would probably get traumatized.

…This one's… good, for sure, but it's more like a political drama than an actual mecha battle anime. It'd probably go over their heads for the most part.

I guess a simple one is probably better. Oh, how about this one… It's less of a mecha anime and more about plastic models instead. It's a pretty relaxing show, and it's quite fun too. It also has a lot of robot model designs, so I'm sure it'll make Doctor Babylon happy… Though I'm not so sure if it'll help them come up with any new tech.

I projected the screen into the air with [**Mirage**] and began playing the show. Then, I left them to their own devices.

"Ohhh, they're watching one of those annie mays? That makes sense…" Yumina had been curious why Linze, Sakura, and Sue hadn't shown up for afternoon tea.

Cesca was up there watching too, so Renne came in to refill our tea.

"…Wish I could've watched too…" Lu grumbled softly as she reached out for a cookie. She was quite the budding anime fan.

Lu was making cookies for the afternoon tea when Doctor Babylon called her, so she couldn't come up to watch with the others.

"I'll send the shows to your smartphones later, okay?"

"Oh, really? Thank you!"

"That's rather convenient. This thing here… We can share information between devices instantly. I can imagine it being useful for world leaders to share or read news…" Leen murmured as she played around with her smartphone. I wasn't quite sure we'd be able to make great use of info-sharing, since less than a hundred people had smartphones.

Then again, since most of those people were world leaders, I had access to information from them pretty easily. They were probably only giving me information they'd been cleared to share, though.

"In the world I came from, regular citizens had access to news from all over the world. You could even find out stuff about individual peoples' daily lives if you wanted."

"Wh-What? Were the citizens constantly monitored or something?" Lu looked almost afraid of the idea.

"No, no… Nothing like that! It was information that people voluntarily gave up. Like, uh… if you decided to write something like 'These cookies are really tasty!' on a certain platform,

195

then anyone with a smartphone would be able to see what you wrote, friend or stranger."

"I-I wouldn't mind if that happened, I suppose… But isn't it scary to know a total stranger could learn things about your life?"

"Yeah, a bit. That's why sensible people don't share too much. Most people only write things that they're happy with other people knowing, but some overshare…"

I could probably make some kind of social network in this world, but I'm not sure how well the people would adapt to it…

You'd often see it online, someone posting something like, "I'm objectively right," only to immediately get flamed by someone saying, "This is literally wrong. It's so wrong you should feel bad." I didn't really want arguments like that to break out between users in this world. Especially not if it escalated to fights breaking out between countries based on shitposting.

I guess a blog would be a better start… Actually, yeah, that's a good idea.

"Hey, Lu. Would you be interested in starting a cooking blog?"

"A cooking what?"

"You can take pictures of the food you make and post them to a special virtual space with instructions on the recipe and stuff. Then others would be able to see and try their hand at cooking on their own. That would allow people from different places to try different dishes that you can show them. Like, uh… if someone from another country decided to look at your blog, they could see a Brunhild-original recipe on there and try making it at home."

Fortunately, the ingredients available on the western side of the world were pretty similar to the ones in the east. That wasn't too surprising, since both worlds were pretty similar.

I was sure that most people would be able to make Lu's dishes, except maybe the more niche stuff. The Grand Potentate of Lassei showed me that his side of the world had rice, too.

"That sounds quite good, yes! We could share dishes from all kinds of countries, not just Brunhild. That would probably bring the people closer together."

"Yes, you're right. We could probably spread Mismede's cully around like that. It might get citizens interested in what the rest of the world has to offer."

Yumina and Leen nodded in approval. Food was often the first step of general interest, so that sounded good to me.

Then again, food worked differently in different cultures. It took a little bit of forcing to get the people of Egret to try eating those Tentaculars, after all. Still, none of the world leaders had any issues with the varied meals I'd served them when they came to Brunhild.

In the end, the blog readers would be able to consult the recipes anyway. It wouldn't be like they were forced to cook everything.

I don't think there's anything I've eaten around the world that I've hated, come to think of it...

Wait... Hold on... That shitty stuff I had back in Yulong! It was that Orc meat char siu rip-off!

Some monsters tasted delicious, like Dragons and Bloody Crabs... Tentacular was also good, depending on the preparation. I personally hated the meat of humanoid monsters like Orcs, but there were probably people who enjoyed it.

"Hmm... Well, I'd like to start with snacks and sides, I think. I can probably manage that, Touya. I'd really like to."

"Alright, let's give it a shot, then."

I borrowed Lu's smartphone and took a photo of the cookies.

"So you could use this photo, then write down the ingredients and the steps for making them. Portion sizes, what utensils you'd need, and so on. Think that'd work?"

"I think so. It's just like learning from the recipes you taught me first, right? I don't have a problem with that."

Ah… Right, I gave her most of the recipes. Maybe I should just look up Earth recipes and then copy and paste them… Oh, wait… The ingredients have different names here. I'll just leave it to Lu.

I think we should consider some special apps. Maybe a [Fireball] app that launches fire if you press a button. That'd be cool… But a touch extreme.

Defensive apps that activated [Shield] or [Reflection] sound good, though!

I decided to think more about this later.

I returned to the lab and found everyone engrossed in front of the anime screen. *Your eyes'll turn square if you stay that close, you know?*

"We need to start developing flight-units! Some kind of simple combination-style one."

"No, ma'am! It has to be a beam sword, ma'am! If we condense magic particles into a specific space, we can turn it into a beam sword!"

"No, that won't do at all! It's gotta be cannons! We could reduce the size of the Brionac and feed it power directly from Babylon!"

"…If we use Gollem G-Cubes as a transmission medium, we should be able to amplify general output."

Welp. Didn't take them long to start brainstorming. Can't you guys just sit back and enjoy the show like Sue?

I was glad that they liked the show, but later on, Sakura kept singing the opening theme over and over. That was a little bit annoying.

Isenberg, the machine city, was once the proud capital of Isengard. But now it was in a sorry state of decline.

Ever since the witch-king fell, nobody was left to bring order back to the place, and thus it lost citizens by the day. There were many political reasons for the exodus, but most people left because of the strange black clouds in the sky.

One day, the citizens of Isenberg noticed black clouds above them. The ominous clouds would often rumble with thunder and spew black rain below. The people viewed it as an omen of death and made haste to depart.

The capital, at this point, was a desolate land. There wasn't really anyone left.

The scout Gollems, Bastet and Anubis, had finally arrived at this forsaken city. They found themselves at a loss when they realized the extent of the carnage.

"Sis… Just what is all this?"

"I can't say for sure… Whatever it is, it's… not right."

The bodies of the dead littered the city streets. Everyone who hadn't fled was now a corpse on the ground. The departed had twisted expressions of anguish painting their faces. Oddly, there were no signs of injury on any of them.

The bodies were strewn about in all kinds of places. Some were on stairwells, others slumped over dining tables, others fallen on park benches. It was as if they'd all died suddenly during their daily routines.

But the strangest thing of all was the condition of the bodies. There were no signs of decay. It looked as though they'd only died about an hour earlier.

But Bastet knew that this couldn't be possible. The clothing on the bodies was frayed and weathered, evidently exposed to the elements for a long period.

All they could deduce from this was that something here was terribly wrong.

"Was it a disease, maybe?"

"Maybe, but we shouldn't jump to conclusions. Let's investigate."

The black dog and black cat dashed up to the top of the tallest building in the city, the Isentower.

The royal castle had previously been the tallest building, but it was destroyed when the witch-king went haywire.

The two scouts figured climbing up to the top of the Isentower would give them a vantage point. The doors to the tower were closed, but that didn't exactly mean much to the duo. Their claws were fashioned from crystal materials even more potent than orichalcum, so the entrance gave way to a few simple swipes.

The noise was incredibly loud as it rang out into the desolate city… but nobody came to investigate. It seemed there were no survivors holed up in the tower.

The two animals began ascending the black iron stairwell. They'd seen from the outside that the top of the tower was home to an enclosed viewing platform, so they continued higher and higher.

When the two made it to the top, they approached one of the windows on the viewing platform and looked down upon the city.

From there they saw the sprawling city streets, the black clouds in the sky, and… it.

"…Just what in the world is that?" Anubis muttered, almost fearful, prompting Bastet to turn and look his way.

The two of them had eyesight far beyond humans. In fact, their sight was better than that of regular cats and dogs as well.

Hell, the distance they could see at would even give an eagle a run for its money. And, with those camera-lens eyes of theirs, they looked far to the south of Isenberg. There, they saw a great mass of gold that dominated the landscape.

The mass of gold was composed of pencil-like pillars that jutted out of the ground. A cluster of massive, muddy crystals.

Bastet didn't see this as some randomized formation. From her point of view, the sprawling structure almost resembled a crystal palace.

"What should we do, sis? Do we investigate over there?"

"…No, I don't think that's wise. Look at the area around it. If we got too close, it would be very dangerous."

"Huh? What? Wait… Augh! Th-That's so gross…"

Anubis refocused his gaze, looking around the crystal mass. He couldn't help but notice that part of the formation on the ground was moving. He increased the magnification of his vision and realized what he was looking at. Skeletons. Numerous muddy-gold human skeletons, marching in formation as if in an unconscious trance.

"There are too many there for us to try getting past. We're running out of time, anyway. We need to head back, or we won't be able to meet with the Grand Duke at the designated hour."

"Ohh, okay!"

"Our job is to extract information, remember? If we overreach and end up being unable to report back, all our work here will have been for nothing. Let's conclude our mission here and now, and then return to Brunhild."

"Okey-dokey." The two animals turned and began walking down the cold iron stairs of the Isentower.

"A golden palace?"

It definitely looked like one. It was sort of in the shape of an upside-down T-piece from Tetris.

I grumbled a bit as I watched Bastet's footage on my smartphone. I'd had a feeling things were going to get annoying… I just wished I hadn't been so right.

"Do you think the wicked god might be in there?" Yumina muttered a question as she snuck a few glimpses at the footage.

"If Karen and the others are right, then probably. When that meteor storm happened, that mass probably landed in Isengard with the other projectiles and started spreading the venom out across the land. Bet it's trying to keep us away while it gestates or something. Doesn't look like it's awake yet, though…"

"I suppose those golden skeletons are people who had their souls devoured…? They're a bit different though, aren't they? Are they mutants too?" Leen murmured to herself as she stroked her chin.

The mutants hunted people with strong negative feelings and sent their energy to the wicked god. Those who had their souls devoured turned into crystal zombies and would go on to attack others.

Those skeletal monsters now had the same muddy-gold color as the other mutants, so it was likely they'd taken on their properties entirely.

Most of the people left in Isenberg probably had their souls devoured and would soon join the marauding army of bones seen by Bastet and Anubis.

"So what are they doing, anyway? Just looks like they're scuttling around to me."

"They might be defending the palace as an army force or something like that... Sure, we couldn't approach due to the divine venom, but it's not like regular adventurers can't go and investigate."

As I answered Sue, I took quiet solace in the fact that I had opted to send the scouting Gollems instead of any adventurers or soldiers. They could've gotten hurt.

"If the capital's already in that state, then I imagine there'll be more refugees..." Yumina was right. The number of people fleeing Isengard to countries like Lassei, Strain, and Gardio had been increasing.

Isenberg was located to the south, so the northern regions weren't as chaotic yet, but obviously, people fleeing from the south were heading up there. And so, they all ran through in a panic.

This panic would then set in through the areas they ran past, causing northerners to want to leave as well.

Most of the refugees were quite financially well-off, too.

Lassei, Strain, and Gardio couldn't just accept anyone into their borders. In order to live, you needed money. That meant that villages and townships were more than happy to accept rich refugees into their folds, but the poor weren't extended the same luxury.

They'd either waste away after being rejected homes or turn to robbery. If you thought about it that way, it was highly possible staying in Isengard would have been a better fate.

If the situation got any worse, I had a feeling there'd be even more civil unrest...

"How's Kousuke doing with the anti-venom plant rearing?"

"It seems like he's making some progress, but it's slow."

Bastet and Anubis had brought back some dirt and rocks that had been soaked in divine venom. I passed them on to Uncle Kousuke. He said he was going to run some tests, but I was a bit concerned.

When I held one of those contaminated rocks in my hands, a sickly, paralyzing feeling ran right up my body. It wasn't bad enough to make me faint, but it kind of felt like I was holding animal guts… Or maybe holding a human brain in my hands. It just felt repulsive, I didn't like it at all.

Since Kousuke had a purer divinity, I was a bit worried that the effects on him would be worse.

I decided to head east of the castle to check up on the guy. He'd set up a research facility there. Though, referring to it as a facility was a bit of a stretch. It was just a vinyl greenhouse made up of thin, clear membranes harvested from magical beasts.

There were various saplings in the greenhouse, as well as various labels and notes in front of each one.

Kousuke himself was standing in front of a plant a bit further inside.

"Howdy, lad."

"Hello, Grand Duke!"

Anubis was lounging around by Kousuke's feet. They both greeted me.

"What's Anubis doing here?"

"I'm totally helping!"

"Aye, I can't exactly touch the contaminants all that much, y'know?"

That made sense.

The sapling in front of Kousuke was around thirty centimeters tall. I wondered if that was the best cultivation he'd gotten so far.

"Lad, y'heard've photosynthesis before?"

"Huh? Sure I have. It's, uhhh… that process where plants take in light and use it to convert water and carbon dioxide into oxygen, right?"

"Well, in layman's terms, aye. The seedlin' here has somethin' goin' for it in a similar vein… It'll filter out the bad venom stuff, an' spew out harmless magic particles."

Oho! That's some impressive purification skills! Looks like that pollution is gonna be toast!

"But… we got a couple problems with it. Anubis, give it another shot."

"Yepperoni!"

Kousuke backed off slightly, and Anubis triggered the **[Storage]** on his collar. A rock, roughly the size of a closed fist, dropped out. The rock landed right next to the sapling.

I could tell at a glance that it was steeped in divine venom. Even just looking at it made me feel a bit queasy.

"Take a gander with yer divine sight."

I followed Kousuke's instructions and glanced over again with divinity clouding my vision. I could see a dirty-looking aura clinging on to the rock, but it was slowly and surely being sucked away.

At the same time, the sapling started accumulating that dirty aura around itself, so it was clearly absorbing the venom. After a short time, the aura spurted out of the plant's leaves and turned into a glittering spray of harmless magical energy. It looked like a complete success to me.

"That's amazing! So if we plant these around Isengard, we can…"

"Hold yer horses, kid. Look closer."

"Huh? Oh…"

The sapling began to rapidly wilt. There was a tiny amount of venom still inside it, and it killed the plant from the inside. The soil around the plant then darkened, and the venom spread.

"If it can't convert all the venom, then there ain't no point. Hell, it could even make the nasty stuff more potent. This plant ain't near proper yet."

Kousuke sighed, prompting Anubis to dig up the polluted dirt. The dutiful dog stashed the soil, along with the dead plant, in his **[Storage]**.

I picked up the rock and was a little shocked to feel nothing from it. The divine venom inside it had been completely purified, so the only problem was getting the plant to do the rest.

"Think you can perfect the plant?"

"Aye, I reckon so. If I brought out the full scope've my divinity, I reckon I could do it real fast… But y'know I can't. It ain't impossible fer me to do it in this sealed form, so I'll just keep perseverin'."

Kousuke's power as a god was pretty intense, so I didn't doubt what he was saying. Unfortunately, in his human form, he'd have to take a long way around. It was just a matter of trying over and over again.

I had hope for him. With the power of the alchemy lab and the spirits on our side, I knew we'd get a purifying plant finished eventually.

"Sorry for the hassle. I'm rooting for you."

"Ain't a problem, son. I'll admit there's a little bit've fun in testin' like this. Can't exactly do this kinda stuff back home, an' all. Don't worry about me, I'm plenty fine with this job."

Kousuke nodded gently, flashing me a peaceful smile. I still felt a little bad, though… This world was only one of many, and it wasn't really their responsibility. I was glad they thought well enough of me and this world to stay and help it.

I talked a little bit more with Kousuke about agricultural plans, but my smartphone started vibrating so I cut the conversation short. It was a call from the king of Belfast. I wondered what he wanted.

I hope you aren't calling just to talk about Yamato again... I know you're happy to be playing with him or seeing him babble and stuff, but you don't need to update me every time he rolls around in a funny position during naptime... Well, whatever. I should stop monologuing internally and pick up.

"Heyo. What's up?"

"Ah, Touya? I'm sorry to trouble you, my boy. Could you swing around to my castle? We've found something odd that we'd like your input on."

"Odd?"

"I've a feeling you may recognize it once you see it. Sorry, again, but you really should come..."

I was a little puzzled. It didn't sound urgent in a dangerous way, so I wondered what it could be... And so, I decided to head over to Belfast Castle.

I opened up a [Gate] and made my way to their royal courtyard. Duke Ortlinde, who was both Sue's dad, and the king's brother, came to escort me with a group of guards.

"What happened?"

"It's less of a 'what happened?' kind of situation, and more of a 'what is this doing here?' scenario..."

The duke caught me up to speed as we walked together. Belfast Castle was surrounded by the castle town to its east, west, and south. Lake Palette was found to its north. It was a water source for the people of the capital, and access was restricted to the general public. The large reservoir of water was effectively royal property.

A short time ago, a lone-horned shark somehow made it into the lake. Apparently, this wasn't too odd and happened once every few years.

The royal family immediately sent out the knight order to slay it. But, in the process of killing it, its horn broke off and sank into the lake depths.

Obviously, they didn't want to waste such a valuable spoil, so one of the knights offered to make use of his diving skills. He went in to fetch it, but he found something else as well.

"We found it, deep within the lake! I never would've guessed it to be there."

"Found what, exactly?"

"You'll know it when you see it..." Duke Ortlinde opened up a door as he spoke.

We passed through the door, which led toward the lake. Its surface shimmered beautifully as we trotted to the lakeside.

Eventually, I made out a few people by the side of the lake. The king was among them.

"Ah, Touya! Over here!"

The king waved over to me. They were gathered around something. As we got closer, I realized what it was. I walked faster. It couldn't be... But it was.

"There's no way... You found this in the lake?"

My voice was barely a whisper. I couldn't believe what I was seeing. After all, the object on the ground was around the size of a small child. It was humanoid... a Gollem. But not just any Gollem. It had the distinct features of a specific production line.

I crouched down and took a look at its neck. There, I saw the mark that confirmed what I already knew. It was a crown.

"There's no other possibility here. This is the white crown."

It looked remarkably similar to Norn's Noir, and Nia's Rouge. It was caked in so much algae and muck that I could hardly call it white, but that was what it was.

"So it is, then... But why is it in our country? Why is it in the royal lake?"

"I have no idea. But around a thousand years ago, a Phrase attack on Belfast may have been stopped by the black and white crowns. It may have shut down then and been here the whole time."

The ruins underneath the old Belfast capital had the language of the Arcana Clan there. It made mention of a black knight and a white knight. I felt like that was referring to Noir and this one.

Welp. Guess I'll see if I can activate it... I placed my hand on the Gollem's chest and channeled some of my magic into it.

"Open."

The soldiers took uneasy steps backward when the Gollem's hatch hissed open. I didn't think it was that scary.

The gel container was there as usual inside the chest cavity, with the G-Cube rotating itself around and gently emitting green light.

I reached out my fingers to touch the G-Cube, but the moment my skin made contact with the gel, something happened.

"Error: Unauthorized, incompatible contact. Current State: Sleep Mode. Initiate R-SEQUENCE. Initiating Self-Preservation Sequence."

"What?!"

A strange, mechanical voice called out from inside the Gollem. My vision went white.

.

..

...

....

"Hm?"

"Uh?"

"What's going on? Woof. What're you two quiet for?"

I blinked my eyes, only to find Kousuke and Anubis in front of me.

I glanced around in confusion. I was inside Kousuke's greenhouse, a stone in my hand. It was the rock that had been purified by the plant back when I was visiting. I was really confused. I was in exactly the same position I was in earlier. Had it teleported me away?

"Hmph. I see, lad. Looks like things just got changed... Goodness me, boy. I reckon y'better calm down an' get yer bearings."

"Huh? O-Okay?"

What does he mean by that? Things got changed? Does he know what happened? Wait, why am I even here? What happened with the white crown?

My head was spinning with so many questions that I had to stop myself. Kousuke had just told me to calm down, so I decided to heed his advice.

"So, what happened jus' now is this... Reality got overwrote, somehow. Ain't got no idea who did it. D'ya?"

"Huh? What? I mean... I don't get it, but..."

I talked to Kousuke about everything that had happened after I left him to his plants. I couldn't really explain everything too well due to my disorientation, but I got through it. I just hoped he could shed some light on what happened.

"Alright, now I getcha. That white crown thinger went an' did this, fer sure."

"Sorry... What exactly did it do?"

"Well, iffin' I wanted to put it simply... I guess it made nothin' happen."

"It... what?"

I was baffled. How could it make nothing happen? What did that even mean?

"So... cause an' effect exists, right? For somethin' to happen, somethin' gotta come before it. You can call that a divergence or turnin' point."

"...Right."

"So, fer example, if you hadn't met little Sue, you wouldn'ta met Duke Ortlinde. Then you wouldn'ta met Yumina. Y'get it?"

"Mostly, yeah."

I only met Yumina because I knew the duke, after all.

"An' without you leavin' Reflet for the capital at that exact time, you wouldn'ta met Sue neither. Hell, you wouldn'ta met Yae neither. If even a single thing in the sequence went different, we prolly wouldn't be havin' this conversation."

...Yeah, guess that makes sense. If God Almighty hadn't made that screw-up, I'd probably be living a regular high school life in Japan right now... Wait, hold on...

"Then are you saying the white crown changes history?"

"Somethin' like that, aye. It ain't the same as turnin' back time, though. It's more like it took the stuff that led certain things to certain places, and made nothin' happen instead. It punched out a piece've the journey. I guess callin' it a reset would work for simplicity's sake. It ain't strong enough to affect the cognitive senses've us divines, though. That's why y'still got yer memories, an' that's why from my perspective things got rewound."

Kousuke quickly glanced at Anubis. The dog was just sitting around like nothing strange had happened, so he was clearly unaffected by the rewind.

It wasn't like time had been reversed; it was just that a new time replaced it. Kind of like resetting in a game. It made it so your loss didn't happen. You could just keep on resetting until you got the desired outcome. If that kind of power was the one that Albus, the white crown, held... I was seriously worried.

"Hm... But wait, I don't think it's resetting to a divergent world, or else it'd just move its master and itself. Nobody else should be able to affect that. So I guess it's like it takes an event from this world, and pulls the possibility of that never happening from a parallel potential world. Then, it patches that onto the current reality, altering the course of events. It's like sewing over a pair of pants to cover a rip, or smoothing over a broken tree branch. Thus, the hole in the pants and the broken tree branch would no longer exist, rendering them gone. Then anything changed by the missing event would change in sequence."

That made it the perfect counterpart to Noir. If the black crown could manifest things from parallel realities... Then the white crown could pull in null points from parallel realities, using them to overwrite events in this world. That reminded me of what the blue crown, Blau, had told me.

"The white crown, Albus, is a special model. It is designed as one of a pair, complementing the black crown, Noir. It is the ultimate folly, one that will bring all reality to naught."

That made more sense now. It was a power that could easily bring reality to naught… Or rather, simply make it so reality didn't happen.

The black and white crowns certainly had similar powers. The black created possibilities from nothing and the white created nothing from possibilities.

"I'm willin' to hazard a guess here. But the white crown prolly caused the reset 'cause it didn't want ya fiddlin' with its G-Cube. It was in sleep mode, aye? That meant it prolly didn't have enough power to do more'n reset the event that led to it bein' found. Course, that power didn't fully work on you."

I listened to Kousuke, nodded, and then called up the king of Belfast.

"Ah, Touya? What do you need?"

I learned from the king that the lone-horned shark had been defeated. Just as Kousuke had assumed, they hadn't found the white crown either.

I asked for more details about their shark hunt, and one detail stood out as different.

The monster's horn hadn't broken off. The white crown must have overwritten this event because it led to the knight diving in and discovering it below the water.

"Touya, lad. Go an' dive into Lake Palette yerself. I reckon the white crown should still be in there. So long as y'don't try to touch the G-Cube, it shouldn't run any resets. That bein' said, I don't reckon it'll have enough power to do another one so soon."

I took Kousuke's advice and opened a [Gate] to the lake. There was nobody around. It seemed like the shark-hunting crew had finished up.

I ran search magic over the lake, but no results came up. I had no idea why that was, but I knew the white crown had to be in there.

"[Prison]."

I formed a translucent blue cube around me, setting it to let oxygen pass through and deny water. And then, I walked into the lake.

I was pretty impressed by the quality of the water. It was so clear I could see a considerable distance ahead of me. It certainly explained why the royal capital was so renowned for its beautiful lake.

"I can see far, but... this is way too much lake... I don't even know where I should start. I should've asked the king where the horn fell before the reset, but I got too excited about the crown. Ah well, how about this..."

I invoked Summoning magic, calling upon Sango and Kokuyou from Brunhild. The heavenly beasts floated by my side.

"Can you guys ask the fish in this lake to look for a white Gollem... Or anything weird like that around the bottom of the lake?"

"As you command."

"Of courssse, darling." Sango and Kokuyou swam around outside the **[Prison]**. I couldn't exactly hear them, but they seemingly shouted off into the water. Before long, a massive amount of fish started gathering nearby... *Man, sometimes I forget you guys have such incredible mastery over animals. It's pretty damn cool...*

Sango and Kokuyou barked further orders, and the fish immediately scattered. Or at least, I hoped they scattered because of the orders. They might have been able to tell from the look on my face just how delicious-looking I thought they were...

We waited on the spot for a while, but eventually, a few fish returned and communicated something to the duo.

"They've found sssomething. Follow them."

It had happened faster than I'd expected. I started to walk along the bottom of the lake, following the trail led by Kokuyou and the school of fish.

Eventually, I came across something half-buried in the depths. I couldn't tell what it was at first. It kind of looked like a weirdly-shaped, algae-covered rock.

I reached down to touch it, and some of the muck gave way. It revealed a white sheen beneath.

I uncovered more of it, wiping it down as I went. It was Albus, the white crown.

No wonder my search magic couldn't find it. It was practically unrecognizable at a glance. The knight who found it before the reset probably bumped into it by mistake or something.

That being said, it was in perfectly good condition for something that had probably been here for such a long time. I wondered if it was because Lake Palette had such clean waters.

Lake Palette wasn't an endorheic basin like Lake Mashu in Hokkaido, so it had other water sources connected to it. And because of that, I figured the lake was probably so clean due to the presence of spirits or something.

Either way, I'd found my mark. I pulled Albus up to the surface with **[Levitation],** opened up a **[Gate],** and headed straight back to Brunhild with the Gollem in tow.

"This is definitely the white crown... I never would've expected it to be in this world..." I'd taken Albus to Babylon's research laboratory, and Elluka started investigating the Gollem right away.

"Hmm... It certainly looks like Norn's Noir. Let's open this bad boy up!"

Just as Doc Babylon was about to crack open the little Gollem like he was a cold one, I grabbed her by the nape of her neck.

"Gaugh!"

"Hold it. I'm not letting another reset happen. You need to listen to me before you do anything."

"Reset?"

Both Elluka and Babylon looked at me in confusion, but they quickly turned to their thinking faces once I explained what had happened.

"The ability to overwrite events, you say? That's certainly similar to what Noir can do... But this is a beastly power that could be used to cause so much more carnage..."

"How do you mean?"

"Don't you understand? Even if there are conditions to use it, the power to turn events into nothing is something obscene... It could cancel out attacks used against it, or remove elements from the past that caused the battle to begin with. But what if that power was used on a person... or even a country?"

"The power could be used to prevent that person from ever being born... Or to stop a country from being founded... The repercussions could be immense. We'd never know."

Elluka's words sent shivers up my spine. It'd be like that cliche in time travel stories where the main character's parents never ended up getting together.

If the meeting between two parents was shifted to an event that never happened, then obviously their kids wouldn't ever be born.

"That being said, I think that's too strong. I doubt it can rewrite things that far away in the past."

"Indeed, I concur. Not to mention the fact that Albus is a crown Gollem. That means there's a price to pay for that power. It has no master, so I doubt it'll be able to make use of the reset anymore... But I do have to question just what the price for its power is. I know in Noir's case, its master has their current life reversed to an extent..."

The white crown's price might have been a hefty one as well. It could probably end up life-threatening if over-used. If it was the opposite of Noir's, then maybe it cut the user's lifespan or something.

"Actually, Touya... If the first discovery of the white crown was undone, then why do you remember it?"

Crap. Why do you have to be so observant, Doc?

I hadn't told anyone but my fiancees about my divine predicament, so I wasn't really sure how to talk my way out.

"G-Guess it's just one of those things? Haha..."

"Hmm..." Doctor Babylon narrowed her eyes at me. She definitely suspected something was up.

"Well, whatever. What do we want to do with the little white guy?"

The easiest solution would be destroying it before it caused any trouble, but I didn't really want to do that. I still didn't know for sure, but I had a fairly high suspicion that Albus was the one that repaired the world barrier way back five-thousand years ago, and again a thousand years ago.

It probably made the event of the boundary line being torn into something that never happened.

If it had that kind of power, then I'd want to make use of it to fix the boundary again.

As it stood, the world was completely undefended due to the recent merger. We'd be utterly defenseless if future invaders like the Phrase wanted to come for us.

"Can we restart it without going for the G-Cube?"

"It's probably a self-defense process that prevents you from wiping its master's info. We should be able to wake it up, so long as we don't try to overwrite its master registry. But that'll mean dealing with an active Gollem that has no master holding it back. If it ends up going out of control, well…"

"We'll have no choice but to fight back, huh. Even destroy it in the worst case…"

At least the "out of control" would just be a regular rampage, instead of its reset function going haywire.

There was a chance it could register us as enemies after awakening, and we wouldn't have its master around to tell it anything to the contrary.

"Worst case scenario, I'll just put it in a [**Prison**]."

"Fair enough. That sounds safe. Who knows? It might be completely docile…" Doc Babylon shrugged.

"Alrighty, let's get this party started."

"Hold on. We should bring Norn here first. Noir might be able to restrain Albus or at least communicate for us."

Elluka's suggestion made sense. Reuniting the white and black crowns after a thousand years sounded like it could be interesting, too.

I couldn't call Norn to Babylon, and I didn't want anything up there getting trashed, so we headed to the training field north of Brunhild castle.

I explained the general gist of the situation to Norn, as we made plans to reactivate Albus.

"Geez, you seriously just happened to find another crown like that? I don't get you at all."

"White…"

Norn sighed in disbelief, while Noir simply stood quietly in front of Albus. Even if it had no memories, it probably had feelings about the situation.

"Open."

Elluka opened up the chest compartment, just as I did before the reset.

The G-Cube rotated around within the gel, softly emitting green light.

Elluka didn't touch the G-Cube. She reached around and pulled out a small stick-looking part from behind it. It kind of looked like a fuse.

"Can you fill this up with magic for me? If Regina and I did it, it'd take us too long."

"Huh? Sure, I guess."

I held the tiny object between my thumb and forefinger and channeled some magic power through it. It ended up taking in a lot of my power. After a while, a little light on it activated.

It looked like it was full, so I handed it over to Elluka. She promptly installed it back into Albus. She took out a screwdriver-like tool and used it to push a button inside. The G-Cube briefly sped up its rotation, but soon returned to normal.

"That should do it."

Elluka closed up Albus' chest hatch, then poured in a little more magic power.

A slow whirring sound began coming from the little machine, and I heard a few clicks and clacks from the insides.

"Crown Series: Model CS—01, 'Illuminati Albus', initializing."

A similar robotic voice to the one I'd heard the last time rang out and the Gollem's visor opened. It began slowly looking around.

Albus gradually rose to its feet. It turned to face Noir, nodding its head gently.

It stepped toward Noir, but stumbled over its own feet.

"Ah…" Albus began speaking, still on the ground.

The white crown fell to the ground and smacked its head right in front of us.

"Fallen… My functions are still not calibrated… Unfortunate…" Noir replied.

"…You have only just reactivated. This is within the parameters of acceptable behavior."

"Comfort unnecessary. My feelings are already damaged."

"Understood."

…Well, it sure doesn't feel like it's gonna randomly attack us out of nowhere.

"Alright, well. My name is Mochizuki Touya. I'm the leader of Brunhild, that's the country we're in. You're Noir's twin model, right? Albus?"

"That is correct…" Albus answered promptly. Seemed like it was willing to communicate.

"Can you tell me your master's name?"

"My master is the King of Belfast, Arthur Ernes Belfast."

"What?!"

Belfast?! Hold on, that's too big a bombshell to just drop like that!

"Hm? What's this mean? Is King Belfast its master?"

"No, he can't be. The current King of Belfast is named Tristwin Ernes Belfast. It's not the same person."

Norn seemed confused, so I quickly explained. It was only natural I'd remember the name of my future father-in-law.

King Tristwin only had one brother, and that was Duke Ortlinde. I also knew for a fact that Sue's dad was called Alfred, not Arthur.

There were only four people in the world right now with the Belfast name... And that was Yumina's direct family.

Her father, Tristwin... her mother, Yuel, Yumina herself, and her little brother Yamato. I'd never heard of any Arthur Belfast.

"Are you sure your master is named Arthur?"

"Affirmative. Arthur Ernes Belfast is my master, and the black crown's master."

"Negative. My master is Norn Patolakshe."

"... Information conflict registered."

Noir shot down Albus' claim. Albus didn't seem to have much to say in response.

If what Albus was saying was true, then this Arthur guy was the master of the black and white crowns... But in that case, how did the black crown end up in an abandoned mineshaft in the Reverse World, and how did the white crown end up at the bottom of Lake Palette?

In fact, why was a Gollem from the Reverse World in Belfast the entire time, anyway? This was so damn confusing.

"Ahh, the Belfast family line did have an Arthur, yes. He was the ruler around a thousand and nineteen years before myself." That was a long time...

I'd called the King of Belfast over the phone, asking him to check his family records. A thousand years ago in Japanese terms would've been the Heian period. Or the time of Fujiwara no Michinaga's rule, in other words.

When I thought about it that way, the technological development of this world was slow compared to Earth... It was something like half the speed. It was probably because of their lack of war, since that was often an instigator for development. Then again, they did fling magic around a lot... Which made them more magically developed.

It wasn't really wise to compare this world to Earth, since Earth didn't have magic or spirits. Lighters weren't necessary if you could just use Fire magic, and you wouldn't need flashlights if you could just cast something like **[Light Orb]**. This world did have lanterns, though... But that kind of stuff had been around since ancient times on Earth, as well.

"Do you know anything about Arthur?"

"Ah, yes. Do you remember the old ruin you found in Belfast a long time ago? He was the king who changed the capital from that old place to the current location."

"I had a feeling."

"The records on Arthur end there, unfortunately. There's no information on these crown whatsits or anything to do with the crystal creatures. Whatever could this mean...?"

King Belfast sighed to himself. He was probably wondering why his ancestor, Arthur, hadn't bothered recording what had happened for future generations to learn from.

I wondered if it was because of a reset canceling things out, but if the Phrase invasion had been nullified, then the capital wouldn't have needed to be moved. It had to be something else.

I thanked the king for his help then ended the call.

"Well?"

"I got confirmation, Doc. There was a king named Arthur in Belfast. He lived over a thousand years ago."

"I see... Hear that, little guy? Your master's long-gone... Unless he was a non-human with a long lifespan, at least."

Doctor Babylon looked over to Albus, but he simply replied with "Acknowledged," which was punctuated by a small beep.

"So what happened a thousand years ago? Hell, what happened five-thousand years ago? Can you tell us, Albus?"

"Negative. Master-level permissions required."

"Your master died a thousand years ago. We can't get those permissions."

"Then cease attempts."

Doctor Babylon shrugged a bit, glancing my way.

...What, she giving up already? This Gollem's surprisingly stoic, but maybe it just doesn't understand the concept of death or something.

I started losing hope until Elluka raised her voice.

"We'll just have to register a sub-master."

"A what now?"

I had no idea what she meant.

"Gollems can't obey anyone other than their masters, but obviously there'd be a countermeasure in place if a Gollem's master died or became incapacitated, right?"

"Right... Because if the master died and the registration remained, then the Gollem wouldn't obey anyone, huh?"

If a Gollem like that went wild, it'd be pretty bad.

"That's why we have a sub-master function installed. If a Gollem recognizes that its master is dead, then anyone with a blood relation to the master can become a sub-master, which is kind of like temporary restricted ownership. Gollems are property too, right? There'd obviously be people who want to make sure their kids get their stuff if they die."

"Ah! Is that kind of how it is with Robert and Blau?"

"That's right. Blau is the Panaches royal family's crown. If a person with the right qualities emerges within the previous master's bloodline, then they can take over full mastery of a Gollem instead of just a sub-mastery. Robert is Blau's full master, but his father and grandfather were only sub-masters. The last full master in the Panaches family was Robert's great-grandfather."

That made sense. If they passed the Gollem down through their family, they could register sub-masters through the generations until a person with the qualities to be a full master appeared.

"That only applies to special Gollems like the crowns, though. Most regular Gollems can be passed from father to son without having to worry about specific qualities. Typically, the previous master's information is expunged after the sub-master is registered, and then the sub-master becomes the full master by default."

That seemed sensible. If a father died, the Gollem would go to his son. I couldn't imagine a Gollem willfully rejecting that course of events.

"So what makes a sub-master different from a regular master?"

"Sub-masters can't use the Gollem skills, for one. The Gollem also becomes less functional across the board."

"So... If Norn died, and Noir was passed down to her kid or something, then the sub-master kid wouldn't be able to use Noir's special ability?"

"Hey, don't just casually talk about my death! I'll smack you over the head!" Norn glared at me just enough to make me regret using her as an example.

Either way, we'd need to use someone who was related to King Arthur of Belfast, a lineage going back over a thousand years.

"... It's Yumina, right?"

"Good job for finally waking up to the obvious. I can't guarantee the sub-master registration will work, since I've never seen a case of a thousand-year gap between registrations, but... They're a royal family, so I doubt their bloodline was thinned too much."

Elluka was right. Cousins often married and reproduced within royal bloodlines in order to preserve the sanctity of their lineage.

Yumina's mother, Queen Yuel, was from a family of nobles that had some Belfast blood as well, so I had a feeling it'd probably be okay if Yumina's bloodline hadn't been too diluted by outside sources. But then again, this was a thousand or so years... That was a crazy number of generations.

"There's no risk to her, is there?"

"None at all. Even if Yumina's fully compatible, she won't be anything more than a sub-master until we wipe Arthur's information and register her in. That means there's no risk of her using one of those dangerous skills she'd have to pay the price for."

If it's safe, then... I guess I'll call Yumina over and explain the current situation. Right now, this is our best lead on some answers.

"Open."

For the second time, or third, if you included the destroyed timeline, Albus' chest was opened up to reveal a G-Cube.

"Is this fine?" Yumina turned back to Elluka, seeking affirmation.

Ordinarily, only a Gollem's master could open up the hatch of an active Gollem. Defensive protocols would prevent any unauthorized person from even trying. Basically, the Gollem would resist with all its might.

But there were two exceptions to this rule. First, the Gollem's creator, the meister, could open it up. Second, a blood relative of a deceased master could open it up.

The fact that Yumina had opened the hatch meant that she had been recognized as compatible and that Albus had registered the truth of its master's death.

"Um... What do I do now?"

"Take a strand of your hair and place it into the G-Cube. That should register you as a sub-master."

Yumina did as she was told, plucking a long strand of her golden hair and feeding it into the sphere around the G-Cube. The cube sucked the hair in, and it began to shine.

"...Looks like it worked. Good job, Yumina. You're Albus' sub-master now."

Elluka smiled as she spoke. I breathed a sigh of relief, since I was half-prepared for another reset to happen.

Thus, the white crown had been passed down from its former master, an event a thousand years in the making.

The hatch closed, and Albus began firing back up with a low hum.

"Crown Series Model CS-01: Illuminati Albus, activating. State name of temporary sub-master."

"Ah… Yumina Ernea Belfast…"

"Registration complete. Sub-master records successfully written. Transferring master control authority from Arthur Ernes Belfast to Yumina Ernea Belfast. Rebooting."

Albus opened up its eyes and started moving once more. Yumina wasn't very tall, but Albus was much shorter. It began intently staring up at her.

After a short while, it bowed down on one knee like a kneeling knight.

"I am the white crown, Illuminati Albus. I pledge my allegiance to you and await your command."

"Thank you. I'm not really sure about how all this works, but it's a pleasure."

"By your command, my lady."

Albus stood back up and gave a firm nod.

Doctor Babylon suddenly stepped forward, clapping her hands together. She had a big grin on her face.

"Alrighty! Now that Yumina's the sub-master, let's get us some answers! Hey, pipsqueak! Tell us everything about five-thousand years ago and one-thousand years ago! I wanna know what happened with you and Noir!"

"Hey, c'mon, Doc. Don't get too impatient."

"Impatient?! Have some mercy, Touya! This is my chance to free myself from the confusion I've had for five-thousand years. I need to know why the Phrase vanished when they did. I need to know how the world was saved when I only foresaw its end... How can't I be impatient and excited when I have the answers right in front of me?!"

When you considered Doc Babylon's circumstances, it was reasonable for her to feel that way. I wanted to know how the white and black crowns repelled the Phrase, too.

"Right, then... Could you tell us who your master was five-thousand years ago?"

"Chrom Ranchesse. He is the meister who created the crowns and the high master of designations white and black."

"I thought as much."

Elluka piped up. It seemed she suspected this. It was plausible that, five-thousand years ago, the master of the white and black crowns would be Chrom Ranchesse, their original creator.

"And what exactly happened five-thousand years ago?"

"Our master, Chrom Ranchesse, used the power of both white and black to travel to another world. After that..."

Albus went on to explain what had happened. I could understand most of what he was saying.

To begin with, Chrom Ranchesse had used the power of the white and black crowns to move from his home in the Reverse World to this world.

This was primarily done with Noir's ability to warp spacetime. It was similar to my ability to warp between worlds with divinity.

It was kind of the opposite of what happened to Lerios Palerius, Primula's founder. If that guy had met with Chrom, he might have been able to make it back home from the Reverse World...

Still, even though Chrom's world-leaping was successful, it came at a great cost. He was an old man when he tried it, but the price to pay reverted his age until he was a relatively young man. If he had screwed anything up or used the power just a bit more, he might have been reverted to a state before he was born.

Albus didn't know why Chrom decided to come to this world. It was possible he was seeking new knowledge, or perhaps simple curiosity. Whatever his reasons, they were now lost to time. I doubted he did it just to become younger.

Either way, Chrom emerged in the part of the world that would eventually become Xenoahs.

Doc Babylon then chimed in to speak.

"Back then, that territory was owned by the United Kingdom of Pillaisula. It was a fairly advanced magi-tech nation, though not as well-developed as Partheno."

Apparently, Chrom settled down in Pillaisula and began to learn from their culture. His Gollems were considered magitech helpers like Babylon's minibots, and thus didn't stand out too much.

Chrom Ranchesse spent ten years living peacefully in Pillaisula. He even had an aptitude for magic. But then suddenly, all hell broke loose.

The Phrase invaded. And when the crystal creatures emerged, the entire world fell into chaos.

The monsters appeared everywhere, killing humans left and right. But to make matters worse, those ancient civilizations were largely magic-based. Their lives were dependent on magical artifacts and daily applications of magic.

You could consider the Phrase a natural predator of civilizations like that. All magic around the Phrase was absorbed and rendered inert. Their regeneration meant that attacks wouldn't keep them at bay for long. The civilizations tried to fight back with magic-fueled tanks and flying airships, but they were all useless.

In the end, cities fell to the Phrase hordes. They were either swarmed by Lesser and Intermediate Constructs or vaporized by the Upper Constructs.

It was during this frightful era that Chrom Ranchesse lived in a frontier village on the outskirts of Pillaisula. He was living his best life. He didn't just have the black and white crowns by his side, but he also had a loving child and beautiful wife.

Chrom sensed the threat posed by the Phrase and desperately experimented with the black crown's power. He wanted to send his family to the world he'd come from, in order to spare them the cruel fate of those who met the Phrase.

But he couldn't work too easily, due to the compensation required to trigger the black crown's ability. Even the meister, who originally created them, was not exempt from the fundamental rule. With great power came great sacrifice.

When he first came to this world, the trade-off was enough to turn him from an elderly man into a young guy. Several years had passed since then, but Chrom wasn't even thirty when the Phrase began their invasion. If he carried out the same spell to send his family back to the reverse world, to safety… he would die.

He attempted, in vain, to design a new crown that could fix things, but it was all for naught.

The Phrase broke through Pillaisula's military line, scattering its armies. They began freely rampaging throughout the country. And, inevitably, the Phrase horde appeared in Chrom's village.

A Dominant Construct appeared with an army. It was masculine in shape, with spiky faux-hair, red eyes, and an arrogant smile.

"Gila, huh…? Guess that bastard was rampaging as he pleased back then, too."

As I listened to Albus talk, I remembered Gila. He was the second Dominant Construct I'd met, the first being Ney. He loved fighting, but was too cocky and destructive for his own good.

Gila was definitely no pushover. Even though I managed to defeat him using my divinity, he was still capable of fighting back against me. My divinity wasn't as well-developed back then, but it was still a serious feat to clash with it.

When Gila showed up in Chrom's village, he started slaughtering people indiscriminately. Didn't matter if they were man or woman, infirm or strong, elder or child. He just enjoyed his hunt.

Chrom tried using the white and black crowns to fight back, but he was still no match for Gila. Given that the crowns couldn't use their special abilities during the fight, it was an obvious loss.

And, after repelling Chrom's attempt at resistance, Gila turned his wrath toward the man's wife and child.

Chrom's family was turned to ashes, incinerated by Gila's particle beam. The resulting despair unleashed by Chrom melded with the abilities of black and white, activating them at the same time.

CHAPTER IV: THE WHITE CROWN

The powers of the black and white crowns were similar, but they functioned differently. When used together, their power went out of control. There was nothing that could stop it.

While the primary component of the combination that brought Chrom across worlds was the black's power, this time the primary component was the power of the white crown. The ability to overwrite reality ran rampant.

This rampant power merged with the black crown's time-related power and began a wave of unusual effects that spread across the entire world.

One of these effects was the world boundary being repaired. Its individual timeline was rewound to a point where it wasn't broken. The aftershocks caused most of the Phrase to be sucked back through to the space between worlds. Then, if I recalled correctly, Ende did something with the Dominant and Upper Constructs.

Several events were grabbed at random from different potential realities and haphazardly pasted over the world in which Chrom had lost his family.

A veritable storm of contradiction began washing over the entire planet. Results occurred, yet the steps were never put in place to achieve them. Successes and achievements were made, yet nobody had put in the work to get there.

For a brief time, utter chaos warped the fabric of reality on a global scale. But the threat, the Phrase, had been wiped from the world. The monsters that had conquered over sixty percent of the planet vanished in an instant.

"Oh, that explains a lot..." Doctor Babylon patted her hands together as if realizing something.

"Hm? What does it explain?"

"Well, on the day the Phrase vanished... I was frantically trying to finalize the Frame Gears. But weird stuff started happening, like uhh... Parts I thought I'd assembled suddenly fell to the floor and started rolling around. Projects and checklists that I hadn't gotten around to were suddenly finished without me doing anything. I thought I was just getting tired, so I brushed it off and went to sleep."

"Do you think that was because of Albus and Noir, then?"

"Yeah, I would think so. Like uhh... Imagine if you had a list that went 1, 2, 3, 4. The power surge from Albus and Noir scrambled that list, then added in other variables like C, or III. So instead of 1, 2, 3, and 4... The list was now like... D, 5, II, and Gamma. It basically made a mess out of causality."

So the power likely dragged in items and events from parallel worlds, replacing existing things with them... That would've definitely confused people on a massive scale.

"I doubt even Chrom would have predicted they'd be capable of that power when combined. He surely would've installed a safety mechanism."

Still, it was probably good he didn't... That kind of raw chaos ended up saving the planet.

Not all the Phrase got moved back to the gap between worlds, but the humans managed to clean up the remaining ones.

"So, wait... What happened to Chrom Ranchesse?"

Yumina looked down at her newly-servile Gollem.

"Master Chrom paid the price for my ability. The white crown, Albus, must be paid in memories. The knowledge he had built up throughout his life. His personal relationships, his love and hate. All was obliterated. That was the price."

"That's awful...!"

So the price for the white crown's power was your memory. The memory of a person was tantamount to their soul. They carried a person's knowledge and feelings.

Albus' power required its master to lose some memories each time its power was drawn upon.

Memories were made every day. Memories were lost every day, too. People never really lost their memory, they just became unable to recall them... If you put it that way, maybe the price wasn't that bad of one to pay.

But obviously, everyone had memories precious to them. Family and cherished friends, dreams, personal achievements, and goals... If they vanished, that'd be a tragedy.

If you thought about it that way, it was the cruelest price of all. Those feelings, those cherished events... They'd just be snuffed out in an instant.

To have long-lasting friendships, or deep and intimate relationships wiped from your mind? It was honestly haunting to think about.

According to Albus, Chrom's memories wouldn't vanish in an instant. They faded away each day, like sand falling through gaps in one's fingers. Little bits of him faded into oblivion, piece by piece.

He protected his wife and child, but his memories of them vanished over time as well, along with all his wisdom and knowledge.

The contradictory waves generated by the white and black rampage even affected the personal histories of the Gollems.

Their G-Cubes were rewritten to the point where their contract with Chrom was rendered as an event that never took place. Without a master to contract with, the two Gollems lost their reason for functioning and powered down.

Chrom never again registered as their master after the incident.

"My functions shut down and I entered sleep mode. I know not what happened to Chrom after that."

With that, the genius Gollem engineer Chrom Ranchesse faded from the annals of history. The price he paid to repair the world was a cruel one indeed.

If, after all that, he lost his memories and became despondent and insane, well… It'd be tragic. But perhaps he'd have been okay with that outcome, since it meant his family survived.

I hoped that he managed to find a new, happier life with his family, even if his memories of their old life vanished. But either way, Chrom Ranchesse and his brilliant mind would be gone. Only a regular, memoryless man named Chrom lived after that.

As for the strange paradoxical events around the world, I had a feeling that people adapted to these things and came up with their own strange explanations over time.

After all, looking at the destroyed towns would be proof that the Phrase had been there… But at the same time, the Phrase were gone.

The only man who could've explained it had an empty mind afterward.

"The white and black rampage, eh? It was quite the coincidental outcome, in the end. I suppose I should thank the two of you, since I lived back then and all… It just kinda feels like the right thing to do."

Doctor Babylon, in a surprisingly timid gesture, bowed her head in sincere apology. I almost wanted to tell her to stop, since it definitely seemed out of character, but I held my tongue.

"So now we know the story of five-thousand years ago. What happened to you two after that?"

"I am unaware. When I was reactivated, I was immediately placed in the service of Arthur Ernes Belfast."

Damn, you just skipped a whole four-thousand years...

That meant we had no idea what Chrom did with the Gollems after the rampage. I wondered if he'd sealed them away, or perhaps sold them to someone.

He'd lost his memories, so it wouldn't be unusual for him to do something like that. After all, the two Gollems would be nothing but strange inanimate objects at that point.

When Albus reawakened, it was apparently within some kind of cave system. Arthur was standing in front of it, along with Noir, who had already been reactivated.

There was a deceased Dragon nearby, and a whole mount of treasure deep within the cave. Apparently, the Gollems had been carried away as part of a Dragon's hoard, and Arthur just happened to find them after slaying the Dragon for its treasure.

Noir had been reactivated first, purely by accident. Its chest hatch just happened to be open within the Dragon's lair, and Arthur had his arm slashed open during the fight. His blood splashed onto the Gollem's G-Cube.

When Noir reactivated, it immediately showed Arthur how to reactivate Albus as well.

By some twist of fate or fortune, Arthur happened to have perfect compatibility for mastery of the Gollems. And he seemed happy to have found such valuable magical artifacts. I could understand why, since having two obedient knights that needed neither food nor sleep was a great boon.

After that, the Gollems faithfully served Arthur for around ten years. Arthur was only a prince when he found them, but he eventually ascended the throne. He was renowned as a brave and wise leader. During that period, Belfast was a fledgling nation with various monsters and magical beasts surrounding its borders. Apparently, Arthur used the two crowns to kill the beasts and expand his national claim.

"Hah. So I guess that means Belfast owes its territory to Albus and Noir…"

"We are owed no debt. We simply followed Arthur."

Well, guess every person has their own history. Although these are Gollems, not really people.

Unfortunately, all was not well for Belfast. One day, Arthur accidentally triggered the black crown's ability. That ability included space-time manipulation and summoning elements from parallel realities and possibilities. That power created a tiny crack in the world boundary.

Arthur had his age reversed a few years as compensation, but the true ramifications of the event would come shortly after. The tiny crack ripped and tore until it became wide enough for the Phrase to pour back through.

It wasn't like the time where the barrier was completely broken. Only about a thousand Lesser Constructs made their way through, but two Intermediate Constructs got through as well.

They appeared overnight in Belfast's capital city, and the army tried to hold fast against them. But the strange crystal creatures were more than a match for the knights, and the city was quickly overrun.

When they fought in formation, they could take on the Lesser Constructs, but the Intermediates were too much of a hurdle. It took the whole army, along with Albus and Noir, just to keep them at a stalemate.

Arthur made a pivotal decision during this war. He decided to use the black crown's power to send the two Intermediate Constructs back through the gap between worlds. If he couldn't beat them, he'd just banish them. It was a simple solution.

It was a success, too. But something terrible happened. Just before the two Intermediates were sent back to the void, they combined their power and launched a railgun strike at the capital.

Arthur acted on reflex, summoning the white crown's power to defend against it. He thought that he could cancel out the attack ever happening... But, because the black crown's power was activated at the same time as the white crowns' again, the two abilities merged and ran rampant once more.

"I have no memories of what happened after this. I fell into sleep mode immediately after."

Albus could only remember seeing Noir get sucked into the gap between worlds, and then itself falling into a nearby lake.

"Hm... So I guess Noir drifted into my world after that? Maybe Noir's lack of memories is because of all that time spent drifting between the two worlds?"

"That's plausible. It would take longer to float across that gap, after all. While Touya and Chrom could cross that sea by boat or plane, little Noir could only float at the mercy of the waves. It's only natural it would take longer."

Elluka and Babylon started pondering together. I turned my eyes toward Yumina, speaking up.

"I wonder what happened to Arthur after that."

"He still exists in our family records, so I imagine he was fine... But the fact that there's no record of his two Gollems probably means their out-of-control power affected the world."

Still, there was still evidence of what had actually happened, like the Arcana Clan's pictographs beneath the old capital.

This was pure conjecture, but I believed Arthur probably lost his memories of the two crowns as the price for using the power. Since the incident wasn't as intense as Chrom's, it probably only created minor contradictions localized to Belfast... In a way, it was like falsifying established history.

"Welp, it's a nice relief to learn about all this... But it sure is a shame old Chrom's knowledge was lost."

Doc had a point, but I thought it was probably okay like this. If Chrom had continued living his life unimpeded, he might've created stronger or more frightening crown Gollems over time.

A contract with a crown always came with a price, after all... It was kind of like making a contract with a devil. There were perks, but it was usually rooted in trouble.

"...Yumina, don't become a full master, okay?"

"I don't even know if I'm fully compatible, but I promise I won't. Were you worried?"

"Well duh. I wouldn't want you to sacrifice your memories."

Yumina giggled softly in response to my words. I pouted, I was being serious! There was no way I'd let Yumina forget her experiences with me and the others.

Hm... If something like that happens, I'll get her memories back. Even if I have to tap into my divinity... Wait, hold on. Yumina's a divine beneficiary, right? Maybe the trade-off won't affect her? Kousuke and I didn't have our memories altered by the reset, right?

Yumina was unrelated to everything that had happened, so it wasn't like she'd have noticed if she was affected or not.

No matter how smart Chrom was, there's no way he could've crafted something that could outdo the gods... I wasn't going to put that to the test, though. It was still possible Yumina could lose her memories.

I reached out to take Yumina by the hand, and she gently entwined her fingers around mine.

"…If you two keep flirting, I'm gonna barf." Norn stared daggers into my back, but I ignored her venomous words. Yumina and I were truly happy.

Here we are again. We're at the end of another In Another World With My Smartphone volume. Did you enjoy the ride?

The battle against the wicked god is coming next volume, and we'll finally see how it ends. Will we finally see the thrilling conclusion to Touya's journey, too? Nope. No way. The series isn't ending next volume. Thankfully, we're still a ways off from the end yet. I appreciate your support along the way.

You might not know this, but the next volume has a special release in Japan that'll come with a Drama CD. This is a follow-up to the Drama CD that came out with the special release of Volume 16. Thanks to everyone's hard work, we managed to get it made pretty fast.

The readers asked for it, and I'm here to deliver. We've even gotten more of the heroines involved this time around.

The previous Drama CD had a reprint, so fans in Japan can still check it out. We're producing more copies for the next volume's release, too.

But since we're only making a little more, I hope my readers in Japan buy it while they can.

The Drama CD has a bath scene, too… If you close your eyes, you might just be able to see it with your mind's eye. Just as good as an illustration, right? No? Fair enough.

Now, time for my thanks.

Thank you to Eiji Usatsuka. Your stuff is as good as ever. I loved the cover illustration of this volume. Seeing Yae struggle to knit was great.

Thank you to Tomofumi Ogasawara. I'm glad that we finally got to portray Lu's Waltraute in a dynamic illustration. Now we've finally seen all of the Valkyrie Gears in illustrated form. I'm happy beyond words.

Obviously, K, and everyone else at Hobby Japan's editorial department. Thank you to everyone involved with this publication.

And, of course, to everyone who supported me on Shousetsuka ni Narou, I thank you as well. Thank you so much.

Patora Fuyuhara

J-Novel Club Lineup

Ebook Releases Series List

* Novel and Manga Editions
** Manga Only

Keep an eye out at j-novel.club for further new title announcements!